NORTH AMER
DONNER PARTY ROUTE:
MISSOURI RIVER
INDEPENDENCE
SPRING-FIELD
WISCONSIN TERRITORY
MICHIGAN
ILLINOIS
INDIANA
OHIO
PENNSYLVANIA
NEW YORK
VERMONT
NEW HAMPSHIRE
MAINE
MASSA-CHUSETTS
RHODE ISLAND
CONNECTICUT
NEW JERSEY
DELAWARE
MARYLAND
VIRGINIA
KENTUCKY
MISSOURI
TENNESSEE
NORTH CAROLINA
SOUTH CAROLINA
ARKANSAS
MISSISSIPPI
ALABAMA
GEORGIA
LOUISIANA
FLORIDA
ATLANTIC OCEAN
GULF OF MEXICO
THE BAHAMAS

NATHAN HALE'S HAZARDOUS TALES
NH HT
SUTTER'S FORT
SIERRA NEVADA
SOUTH PASS
SCOTT'S BLUFF
ALCOVE SPRINGS
INDEPENDENCE
DONNER DINNER PARTY
DINNER PARTY? WHERE'S THE FOOD?
AMULET BOOKS, NEW YORK

CATALOGING-IN-PUBLICATION DATA HAS BEEN APPLIED FOR AND MAY BE OBTAINED FROM THE LIBRARY OF CONGRESS.

ISBN: 978-1-4197-0856-5

BOOK DESIGN BY NATHAN HALE AND CHAD W. BECKERMAN

PRINTED AND BOUND IN CHINA

18

ABRAMS The Art of Books
195 Broadway, New York, NY 10007
abramsbooks.com

TO THE MEMORY OF MY
GREAT-GREAT-GREAT-GRANDFATHER EPH HANKS,
A RESCUER OF SNOWBOUND PIONEERS

SEPTEMBER 22, 1776
PROLOGUE
MANHATTAN, NEW YORK
HEAR YE! HEAR YE! HEAR YE!
HEAR YE! HEAR YE! HEAR YE!
LET IT BE KNOWN THAT ON THIS DAY, *THIS* MAN--
--CAP'N NATHAN HALE!
--*IS SENTENCED TO DIE BY HANGING!*
HANGING!
FOR THE CRIME OF SPYING AGAINST HIS MAJESTY *KING GEORGE!*
WE HANG SPIES!
THAT WE DO, SIR.
CRINKLE
AND HEAR YE! HEAR YE HEAR YE!
HEAR YE?
LET IT *ALSO* BE KNOWN THAT THIS MAN...
...HAS BEEN TELLING THE MOST *AMAZING STORIES!*

AMAZING STORIES FROM HISTORY.
THAT'S RIGHT, BECAUSE WHEN HE SAID HIS LAST WORDS--
LAST WORDS?
"I REGRET THAT I HAVE BUT ONE LIFE TO GIVE FOR MY COUNTRY."
THEM'S THE WORDS!
PROBABLY THE GREATEST LAST WORDS EVER! THEY PUT HIM RIGHT INTO THE HISTORY BOOK!
FROM INSIDE THAT HISTORY BOOK, CAP'N HALE HAS SEEN IT ALL-- THE PAST! THE FUTURE!
THE PRESENT.
AND NOW HE'S TELLING THE BEST STORIES FROM HISTORY!
COME FOR THE STORIES. STAY FOR THE HANGING.
YEAH!
HEAR YE! HEAR YE! HEAR YE!
HEAR YE! HEAR YE! HEAR YE!
CRUNCH CRUNCH
WE CAN'T HANG YOU UNTIL WE GET SOME KIND OF AUDIENCE.

I HAVE MANY MORE STORIES TO TELL.
HOW ABOUT ANOTHER WAR STORY? SOMETHING WITH A GOOD CAVALRY CHARGE!
DON'T START YET. I'LL BE RIGHT BACK.
AMERICAN HISTORY ISN'T JUST WAR STORIES.
SOMETHING WITH HORSES IN IT.
WHERE IS THAT WICKED HANGMAN?
HERE I AM, SIR.
WHAT ARE YOU DOING!?
WHILE HE'S TELLIN' HIS NEXT STORY, I THOUGHT WE COULD HAVE SOME NICE TEA AND BISCUITS.
SCOOT
TEA AND BISCUITS!? ON THE GALLOWS!!?
SIP.
DO YOU KNOW WHAT A GALLOWS IS FOR?!
DIP.
HANGY-HANGY?
THAT'S RIGHT. HANGY-HANGY! NOT SIPPY-SIPPY!
CRASH

THAT WERE ME MUM'S FAVORITE TEA SERVICE.
I'M NOT SORRY.
THERE IS A TIME AND A PLACE FOR TEA PARTIES. THIS ISN'T IT.
BEGGIN' YOUR PARDON, SIR, BUT IT IS TEATIME.
SO IT IS. I AM A BIT PECKISH MYSELF. DO YOU HAVE A STORY, CAPTAIN HALE?
I'VE GOT A STORY ABOUT HUNGRY PEOPLE.
WE ARE HUNGRY PEOPLE-- WE DON'T WANT TO HEAR ABOUT OTHER HUNGRY PEOPLE.
THIS STORY IS GUARANTEED TO MAKE YOU LOSE YOUR APPETITE.
DOUBTFUL, I HAVE A ROBUST APPETITE.
ME TOO! LET'S HEAR THIS HUNGRY STORY.
I AM INTRIGUED. TELL YOUR TALE, CAPTAIN HALE.
SIR?
VERY WELL. SET IT UP. THIS WON'T BE A REAL GALLOWS UNTIL AFTER THE STORY.
GOODY!
THIS STORY TAKES PLACE IN 1846, FAR WEST OF HERE.
OOH! A TALE OF THE FUTURE!
I MUST SAY, FOR A DEAD MAN, YOU CERTAINLY KNOW A LOT ABOUT TOMORROW.
IT IS A TIME OF WESTWARD EXPANSION. PEOPLE ARE LEAVING THE EAST AND MOVING WEST, INTO THE WILDERNESS...
SUGAR, SIR? ONE LUMP OR TWO?
THREE.
AND A FEW OF THOSE BISCUITS.

CHAPTER 1
MARCH 1846
SPRINGFIELD, ILLINOIS
MISSOURI RIVER
ST. LOUIS
PONY! PONY! PONY!
LOOK AT MY BRAND-NEW PONY!
IT'S MINE! I HAVE A PONY!
I HAVE MY VERY OWN PONY!
HELLO, MR. LINCOLN. I HAVE A NEW PONY!
YOU DO?
WHERE IS IT?
RIGHT HERE! I'M SITTING ON HIM!
OH, IS THAT WHAT THAT IS?
HIS NAME IS BILL. I'M RIDING HIM ALL THE WAY WEST--TO CALIFORNIA!
OH? YOUR FAMILY IS MOVING WEST, EH?
YES! AND I'M GOING ON MY PONY!
WHY DOES VIRGINIA GET A PONY? I WANT A PONY.
YEAH! WHERE ARE OUR PONIES?
I WANNA PONY.
PATTY REED, AGE 8
JAMES REED JR., AGE 5
THOMAS REED, AGE 4

YOU YOUNGER KIDS WON'T NEED PONIES.
WE WON'T?
OF COURSE NOT! YOU'LL BE RIDING IN THE WAGON WITH GRANDMA!
I DON'T WANT TO GO TO CALIFORNIA!
HEADING WEST AT LAST, EH, JAMES? AREN'T YOU LUCKY?
YES, INDEED! WE'LL BE HEADING OUT IN A MONTH.
AHH, ADVENTURE! AND HERE I AM, STUCK LAWYERING IN ILLINOIS.
WELL, WE CAN'T ALL MAKE HISTORY, CAN WE, ABE?
HA! NO, WE CAN'T!
HAVE FUN, ALL OF YOU. I'LL MISS MY NOISY LITTLE NEIGHBORS.
BYE, MR. LINCOLN.
BEST OF LUCK, ABE. I HOPE YOUR LAWYER JOB WORKS OUT FOR YOU.
AND I WISH YOU WELL ON YOUR TRIP TO FAR CALIFORNIA.
HEY! WE'VE SEEN THAT GUY BEFORE, IN THE IRONCLAD STORY! HE WAS PRESIDENT!
HE DOES BECOME PRESIDENT-- ONE OF AMERICA'S GREATEST PRESIDENTS, IN FACT. BUT IN THIS STORY, HE WAS JUST A NEXT-DOOR NEIGHBOR.
SILLY LITTLE COUNTRY. I ASSUME EVERYONE TAKES A TURN BEING THE PRESIDENT.

ONE MONTH LATER, APRIL 1846, SPRINGFIELD, ILLINOIS
PONY!
PONY! PONY!
I WISH SHE'D SHUT UP ABOUT THAT PONY.
WE ALL DO, PATTY.
LOOK! DAD'S BACK WITH A WAGON!
COME AND TAKE A LOOK, KIDS!
THIS WAGON IS A PALACE!
IT'S GOT A SIDE DOOR! NOBODY ELSE HAS A WAGON WITH A SIDE DOOR! AND FOUR YOKED OXEN TEAMS! THAT'S EIGHT OXEN!
IT HAS SPRINGY SEATS!
AND A STOVE RIGHT INSIDE!
OW!
AND A MIRROR!
WHEE! LOOK AT ME!
WHY, YOU WON'T EVEN NOTICE THE JOURNEY!
IT'LL BE LIKE SITTING COMFY-COZY AT HOME!
I WANNA PONY.
WHERE DOES THE FOOD FIT?
IN THE FOOD WAGON. WE'LL BE TAKING THREE WAGONS.
HERE COME THE DONNERS!
GEORGE DONNER!
HURRY AND FINISH YOUR PACKING, JAMES REED! IT'S TIME TO GO!

SEE THIS? IT'S 150 POUNDS OF BACON!
PORK
WOW!
THERE'S A FULL BARREL FOR EACH PERSON!
I EAT THAT MUCH BACON EVERY WEEK!
IS ALL OF THIS JUST FOOD?
IT SURE IS! I WON'T HAVE ANY-ONE GOING HUNGRY ON MY TRIP!
THIS ONE'S FULL OF FLOUR -- 200 POUNDS!
I DON'T EAT FLOWERS. I'LL STICK TO BACON.
AND THIS ONE'S FULL OF TIGER REPELLENT.
DID YOU BRING TIGER REPELLENT?
NO.
THEN TIGERS WILL EAT YOU.
THREE WAGONS, A HILL OF SUPPLIES, AND A HERD OF ANIMALS...
JAMES REED, YOU LOOK LIKE YOU'RE PREPARED FOR ANYTHING!
CAN'T BE TOO CAREFUL!
MOM, CAN CASHY RIDE IN THE WAGON?
NO. CASH CAN FOLLOW THE WAGON WITH THE OTHER DOGS!
AWW!
THAT DOES IT! WE'RE ALL PACKED!
READY TO GO!
WOOPS!
I FORGOT ONE THING!
MAKE ROOM FOR GRANDMA!

JAMES AND MARGARET REED FAMILY: 2 ADULTS, 4 CHILDREN, 3 TEAMSTERS, 1 COOK, 1 COOK'S BROTHER, 1 GRANDMA
JACOB AND ELIZABET
2 ADULTS, 7 CHILDREN
VIRGINIA AND PONY
I DON'T UNDERSTAND. WHY ARE YOU SHOWING US SOME FAMILIES MOVING HOUSE?
THEY AREN'T JUST MOVING HOUSE, THEY ARE CROSSING THE CONTINENT.
IN THOSE WAGONS!?
NO ONE HAS EVER DONE SUCH A THING!
NOT IN 1776. RIGHT NOW WE ALL LIVE ON THE EAST COAST, IN THE THIRTEEN COLONIES.
THESE PEOPLE WANT TO CROSS TO THE WEST COAST.
IN 1846, THE AMERICAN POPULATION WILL BE ALMOST FOUR TIMES LARGER THAN IT IS NOW, IN 1776.
UNORGANIZED TERRITORY
MEXICO
1846
1776
TEXAS
THE SIZE OF THE COUNTRY WILL QUADRUPLE TOO.
HOW IS THAT EVEN POSSIBLE?
IN 1803, NAPOLEON BONAPARTE SELLS THE LOUISIANA TERRITORY TO AMERICA.
et voila
BONAPARTE! THAT DEVIL!
OLD BONEY SELLS IT FOR LESS THAN 3¢ AN ACRE.
Bonaparte
CURSE YOU, BONEY!
IN 1804, A COUPLE OF ADVENTURERS NAMED LEWIS AND CLARK WILL LEAD AN EXPEDITION TO SEE WHAT IS IN THE LOUISIANA PURCHASE. THEY CROSS ALL THE WAY TO THE PACIFIC--
3¢ AN ACRE, HUH?
BUT THAT'S ANOTHER STORY.
IS IT DANGEROUS TO CROSS?
IT IS VERY DANGEROUS.
THE INTERIOR OF THE CONTINENT IS FILLED WITH TALL MOUNTAINS, DEEP CANYONS, VAST DESERTS, AND WILD ANIMALS. IT IS PEOPLED WITH INDIAN TRIBES, MANY OF WHOM AREN'T HAPPY TO WELCOME SETTLERS.
AND THEY BROUGHT CHILDREN ON THIS TRIP?
THEY'RE CRAZY!
A LITTLE CRAZY, YES. BUT IN 1846 NEARLY 3,000 PIONEERS GO WEST.
I HOPE NOTHING BAD HAPPENS TO THEM!

DONNER FAMILY:
3 TEAMSTERS
GEORGE AND TAMSEN DONNER FAMILY: 2 ADULTS, 5 CHILDREN,
1 TEAMSTER, 1 SHOPKEEPER, 1 ENGLISH GOLDSMITH
CHAPTER 2
MAY 11, 1846
SPRINGFIELD, ILLINOIS
INDEPENDENCE, MISSOURI
WE'VE MADE IT!
WE MADE IT? WE'RE THERE!?
WE'RE IN CALIFORNIA!?
CALIFORNIA! YAAAAAY!
NO, NO, NO. THIS IS INDEPENDENCE, MISSOURI!
THE JUMPING-OFF POINT FOR THE JOURNEY!
I THOUGHT WE ALREADY JUMPED OFF.
WE'VE BEEN RIDING IN THIS WAGON FOR A WHOLE MONTH--
AND WE HAVEN'T EVEN STARTED YET!?
THIS IS THE LAST TOWN BEFORE WE PLUNGE INTO THE WILDERNESS!
DRY GOODS
SUPPLIES
HARDWARE
LAST CHANCE STORES
YOKES
FEED
SMITH
TRADING

GOOD HEAVENS! THESE PRICES ARE SKY-HIGH!
$10
LUCKY FOR US, WE ARE WELL SUPPLIED.
ONLY A FOOL WOULD BUY THEIR GEAR HERE.
FLOUR $4.00 PER BARREL
HORSES $40.00
BOOTS
PLENTY OF FOOLS OUT TODAY.
DO WE NEED TO STOP HERE AT ALL?
TACK
YES.
IT IS HERE WE WILL JOIN THE GREAT OVERLAND CARAVAN!
A CARAVAN? AREN'T WE GOING ON OUR OWN?
NO, VIRGINIA, DEAR, WE WANT TO JOIN A GOOD WAGON TRAIN.
IF YER LOOKIN' FER A TRAIN, YE SHOULD LOOK FER COL. *WILLIAM RUSSEL*-- HE'S GOT ALPHONSO BOONE WITH 'IM.
ALPHONSO BOONE? WHO'S THAT?
ONLY THE GRANDSON OF **DANIEL BOONE**!
DANIEL BOONE'S GRANDSON! HOT DIGGITY! THAT'S THE TRAIN FOR US!
BETTER GIT MOVIN'. RUSSEL'S ALREADY DOWN AT THE KAW RIVER!
MAY 19, 1846, KAW RIVER, KANSAS TERRITORY
WHY, YES, YOU MAY JOIN MY COMPANY.
THAT'LL PUT US AT FIFTY WAGONS!
HOORAY! IT'LL BE EASY-GOING FROM HERE ON!
BOOOM

MAY 29, 1846
ALCOVE SPRINGS
PLATTE RIVER
BIG BLUE
MISSOURI RIVER
LITTLE BLUE
ALCOVE SPRINGS
KANSAS "KAW" RIVER
INDEPENDENCE, MISSOURI
KANSAS TERRITORY
SARAH KEYES
BORN IN VIRGINIA
WELL, GRANDMA DIDN'T MAKE IT VERY FAR.
NO, SON, SHE DIDN'T.
BUT SHE DIED DOING WHAT SHE LOVED...
RIDING IN A WAGON.
I WANNA GO HOME!
ME TOO.
NOW, CHILDREN...
WHY DID WE EVER LEAVE HOME!?
YOU KNOW WHY, PATTY.
WHY?
FOR FORTUNE, DESTINY, AND GLORY!
THE DISTANT LAND OF CALIFORNIA IS FREE! FREE FOR THOSE BRAVE ENOUGH TO CLAIM IT! THERE ARE ONLY A FEW HUNDRED AMERICAN SOULS IN ALL OF CALIFORNIA! THOSE OF US DETERMINED ENOUGH WILL SET UP MIGHTY EMPIRES OF WEALTH, LAND, AND POWER! ONWARD TO FORTUNE! ONWARD TO GLORY!
ONWARD TO DESTINEEEEEEEEEEEE--
FUNERAL!
UH. YES...
DOES ANYONE ELSE HAVE SOMETHING TO SAY ABOUT GRANDMA?
GOOD-BYE, GRANDMA. WE'LL MISS YOU.
THAT'S RIGHT.
MAY 31, 1846
BIG BLUE RIVER
WE HAVE TO CROSS THAT?

LOOK, IT'LL BE EASY! THE WAGONS WILL CROSS ON THE FERRY!
I DON'T SEE A FERRY, I SEE A FLIMSY LOG RAFT.
IT'S THE BLUE RIVER ROVER! WE BUILT THIS WITH COL. RUSSEL'S MEN!
YOU'LL BE AS SAFE AS CAN BE!
AREN'T YOU RIDING ACROSS WITH US?
GOOD HEAVENS, NO! I'LL SUPERVISE FROM SHORE.
SWIM, BILLY, SWIM!
PULL FASTER, BOYS!
SIX MORE WAGONS NEED TO COME ACROSS!
BOOOM
NOT THE RAIN AGAIN!
GREAT! NOW WE'RE GONNA GET WET!
WATCH OUT! THE THIRD WAGON IS SWAMPING!
SPLOOSH
ENOUGH RAIN! ENOUGH WATER! I'M TIRED OF BEING SOAKED ALL THE TIME!
I'LL TAKE ANYTHING BUT MORE RAIN!

JUNE 2, 1846, TWO DAYS LATER
IT'S F-F-FREEZING!
IT'S JUNE! IT'S SUPPOSED TO BE HOT!
ONE WEEK LATER.
I WISH IT WOULD RAIN!
BILLY DOESN'T LIKE THE HEAT!
CAN HE RIDE IN THE WAGON?
SURE, LET'S PUT HIM UP HERE IN GRANDMA'S BED.
REALLY?
NO.
BUT LOOK AT HIM, HE'S ROASTING!
THEN GIVE HIM A BREAK! HE'S BEEN HAULING YOU AROUND FOR MONTHS!
HE LOVES TO HAUL ME AROUND! HE LOVES ME!
DON'T YOU, BILLY?
WHO'S MY FAVORITE PONY?
FAITHFUL BILLY, HE'S A GRAND PONY.
WELL, CHILDREN, WHAT DO YOU THINK OF THE WILD FRONTIER?
LOOK! TRAPPERS RETURNING TO THE STATES WITH ALL THEIR LOOT!
MEH.
LOOK! A FRIENDLY PAWNEE TRADER!
WHAT'S THAT YOU'RE TRADING, THERE?
BUFFALO TONGUE, YOU TRADE FOR HOGMEAT?
BUFFALO TONGUE? CERTAINLY!
MM-MM-MM-DELITHIOUS!
EWWWWWW!

CHAPTER
3
JUNE 9, 1846
PLATTE RIVER
INDE-PEN-DENCE
LOOK AT ALL THE BONES!
THIS MUST BE AN OLD BUFFALO HUNTING GROUND.
THAT SKULL IS ON A POLE!
CAN WE GO SEE?
YES, BE CAREFUL!
BAD WATER AHEAD 1mile
OOOH! WRITING!
LET'S MAKE SOME MORE!
1mile
Giant Spiders ahead
NO TALKING
MONSTER BATS!
ALL THOSE BUFFALO BONES, BUT NO BUFFALO!
I WANTED TO HUNT BUFFALO! LUCKILY I FOUND AN ELK.
THESE HUNTERS FOUND ANOTHER BONEYARD.
BUT IT WAS ALL HUMAN BONES-- SHOW 'EM, BOYS!
LOOKY THERE! PROB'LY AN INDIAN!
AAAAAAGH!
PUT THAT BACK, YOU FOOL! IT'S BAD LUCK TO DISTURB AN INDIAN BURIAL GROUND!
BAD LUCK?
I HOPE YOU ARE ALL ENJOYING THE ELK STEAKS I PROVIDED.
I HAPPEN TO BE A FORMIDABLE HUNTER.
FOR THIS EVENING'S ENTERTAINMENT, I SHALL TELL YOU THE HEROIC TALE...
...OF HOW I HUNTED AND SHOT THE ELK.
MUSIC! WE WANT SOME MUSIC!
YOU WANT ME TO SING MY ELK TALE?
JAAAAAAAAAMES REEEEED! HE WAS A HEEEEEROOOO!
HE SHOT A MIGHTY EEELLLLLLLLLLLK!
BOOO! SIT DOWN!

THANK YOU, THANK YOU! NOW I'D LIKE TO DISCUSS MY TWO FAVORITE WORDS.
"JAMES REED."
SHORT CUT!
"SHORTCUT" IS ONE WORD.
I'VE BEEN THROUGH THIS BOOK SEVERAL TIMES.
THE EMIGRANTS' GUIDE TO OREGON AND CALIFORNIA ... LANSFORD W. HASTINGS
I'VE FOUND A WAY TO SAVE US 400 MILES OF TRAVEL! HOW WOULD YOU ALL LIKE THAT!?
LET ME READ MR. HASTINGS'S WORDS FROM PAGE 137:
"THE MOST DIRECT ROUTE, FOR CALIFORNIA EMIGRANTS" --THAT'S US!--"WOULD BE TO LEAVE THE OREGON ROUTE,
ABOUT TWO HUNDRED MILES EAST FROM FORT HALL; THEN BEARING WEST SOUTHWEST,
TO THE SALT LAKE;
AND THENCE CONTINUING DOWN TO THE BAY OF SAN FRANCISCO."
TO OREGON
FORT HALL
INDEPENDENCE ROCK
FORT LARAMIE
GREAT SALT LAKE
FORT BRIDGER
CHIMNEY ROCK
THE HASTINGS CUTOFF
SUTTER'S FORT
ALCOVE SPRINGS
INDEPENDENCE
LOOKS LIKE A PRETTY GOOD SHORTCUT!
THEY ARE ONLY HERE? THEY'VE GOT A LONG ROAD AHEAD.
IMAGINE THAT! LEAVING THE OREGON TRAIL--
SHAVING FOUR HUNDRED MILES OFF!
NO MORE WAGON TRAIN DUST!
NO MORE FIGHTING FOR GOOD CAMP-SITES!
IT'S ALL RIGHT HERE IN THIS BOOK--THE HASTINGS CUTOFF!
HOORAY! HOORAY FOR THE HASTINGS CUTOFF!
HOORAY FOR THE SHORTCUT!

JUNE 16, 1846
PLATTE RIVER
BUFFALOES!
BUFFALO AT LAST!
HO THERE, CHILDREN, WOULD YOU LIKE TO GO HUNTING...
YEAH!
...FOR BUFFALO CHIPS FOR TONIGHT'S FIRE?
HA-HA! TALLY HO!
AWW.
COME ON, JAMES. LOOKS LIKE WE'RE ON BUFFALO POOP PATROL AGAIN.
HO THERE, VIRGINIA, WOULD YOU LIKE TO GO HUNTING...
OH BOY, WOULD I!!!
...FOR BUFFALO CHIPS--
UH-OH.
VIRGINIA!
YEEEEEEEEEEHAAA
OH BOY.
WATCH IT, KID! DON'T CAUSE A STAMPEDE!
YIP
YIP
YIP
THEY COULD CHARGE INTO THE WAGONS!
I AM A GREAT HUNTER!
YEEP!
DID YOU SEE THAT!
I AM A GREAT BUFFALO HUNT--
SPLAT

YOU! YOU LITTLE--
I CAN'T BELIEVE YOU DID THAT!!
YOU ALMOST GOT US STAMPEDED!
I'LL GET YOU FOR THIS, PATTY.
NICE SHOT, PATTY.
HE SAAAAAAW THE BUFFAAALOOOOO...
HE TOOK CAREFUL AAAAAAAAAAAIM...
OH, YES HE DID!
I WISH HE WOULDN'T SING.
AND WITH A MIGHTY BAAAAAAAAAAANG...
HERE'S SOME MORE BUFFALO CHIPS FOR THE BONFIRE.
WANT SOME, VIRGINIA?
I WILL GET YOU.
WHY ARE THEY BURNING POOP? WHY DON'T THEY USE WOOD?
WOOD IS HARD TO FIND ON THE GREAT PLAINS. POOP ISN'T.
YOU KNOW, PATTY, WE'VE NOW CROSSED INTO SIOUX TERRITORY. I HOPE NONE OF THEM KIDNAP YOU.
LIKE IN GRANDMA'S SCARY INDIAN STORIES.

CHAPTER 4
JUNE 23, 1846
THERE IT IS, CHILDREN, CHIMNEY ROCK! THE EIGHTH WONDER OF THE WORLD.
ALL I SEE IS DUST.
NO, NO, LOOK PAST THE DUST, SEE THE ROCK?
OH BOY. A ROCK. TOO BAD THE DUST IS RUINING OUR VIEW OF A ROCK.
JUNE, 28 1846, FORT LARAMIE
NIOBRARA RIVER
NORTH PLATTE RIVER
FORT LARAMIE
CHIMNEY ROCK
PLATTE RIVER
IS THAT JAMES REED? PRIVATE JAMES REED?
CLYMAN!? IT CAN'T BE! LIEUTENANT CLYMAN? WHAT ARE YOU DOING OUT HERE?
JUST MAKIN' MY WAY FROM HERE TO THERE.
WE'RE HEADED WEST, LIEUTENANT, ARE YOU?
ME, NO. I'VE ALREADY BEEN WEST, NORTH AND SOUTH TOO.
WHO IS THIS GUY?
AND WHY DID HE SAY "PRIVATE" REED? ARE THEY MILITARY MEN?
YES, THEY BOTH WERE IN THE ARMY, IN A WAR CALLED THE BLACK HAWK WAR.
YEAH! BLACK HAWK WAR! DID THEY FIGHT HAWKS?
BLACK HAWK WAS A MAN.
THE BLACK HAWK WAR IS ONE OF THE FEW AMERICAN WARS NAMED AFTER A SINGLE PERSON.
WOW! WHAT DID HE DO?

HE BLACK HAWK WAR
ONE•PAGE•WAR MINI•COMIC
BLACK HAWK, WHOSE REAL NAME WAS MÀ-KA-TAI-ME-SHE-KIÀ-KIÀK, WAS A SAUK CHIEF.
IN APRIL 1832, HE LED A BAND OF 1,100 MEN, WOMEN, AND CHILDREN ACROSS THE MISSISSIPPI TO RECLAIM LANDS TAKEN BY AMERICAN SETTLERS.
COULDN'T THEY ALL JUST **SHARE** THE LAND?
AN 1804 TREATY SAID NO, THE INDIANS HAD TO GO. BLACK HAWK DIDN'T AGREE WITH THE TREATY. SO HE TOOK HIS BAND, "THE **BRITISH BAND**"--
WHAT? **BRITISH?**
BLACK HAWK HAD SIDED WITH THE BRITISH DURING THE WAR OF 1812.
THE BAND CARRIED A BRITISH FLAG TO SHOW HOW MUCH THEY DISAGREED WITH THE AMERICAN TAKEOVER.
HA! I LIKE THEIR **SPIRIT!**
A MILITIA WAS FORMED TO STOP THE BRITISH BAND.
BOTH JAMES REED AND JAMES CLYMAN JOINED THAT MILITIA.
HEY! I SEE ABRAHAM **LINCOLN** AGAIN!
HE SURE GETS AROUND!
BLACK HAWK HOPED OTHER TRIBES AND EVEN THE BRITISH IN CANADA WOULD JOIN HIS CAUSE.
THEY DIDN'T. THE BRITISH BAND WAS LEFT TO STAND ALONE.
BLACK HAWK ATTEMPTED TO NEGOTIATE A TRUCE AT OLD MAN'S CREEK.
THE UNTRAINED MILITIA SHOT HIS SCOUTS. THE TRUCE BECAME **THE BATTLE OF STILLMAN'S RUN.**
AT THE BATTLE OF WISCONSIN HEIGHTS, A WAR PARTY OF 120 STOOD AGAINST **750** MILITIAMEN.
THEY HELD THE MILITIA OFF LONG ENOUGH FOR THE WOMEN AND CHILDREN OF THE BRITISH BAND TO ESCAPE ACROSS THE WISCONSIN RIVER.
BY AUGUST, NEARLY HALF OF THE BRITISH BAND WERE DEAD.
THEY TRIED TO RETREAT ACROSS THE MISSISSIPPI.
A STEAMBOAT CALLED *THE WARRIOR* ARRIVED, FILLED WITH ARMY AND MILITIA. THE LAST OF THE BRITISH BAND WAS CAPTURED OR KILLED.
BLACK HAWK SURRENDERED.
IN 1976, THE U.S. ARMY NAMED A HELICOPTER AFTER HIM.

WHO WAS THAT? HE SMELLED FUNNY.
AN OLD FRIEND FROM THE WAR.
DOES HE LIVE IN THIS FORT?
HE WILL TONIGHT, AND SO WILL WE.
AFTER FORT LARAMIE, WE'LL GO TO FORT BRIDGER, AND THEN, AT LAST, TO SUTTER'S FORT-- IN CALIFORNIA!
WOO! THREE FORTS TO GO!
FORT! FORT! FORT!
PATTY, YOU SHOULD SEE THESE INDIANS!
THEY HAVE GIGANTIC FEATHER HATS!
TELL ME WHEN WE'RE SAFE INSIDE THE FORT!
WE ARE INSIDE-- SO ARE THE INDIANS.
THE SIOUX HAVE A BIG WAR PLANNED WITH THE CROWS AND THE SNAKES.
YOU BEST KEEP OUT OF THEIR WAY.
CROWS AND SNAKES!
YOU MADE THAT JOKE EARLIER.
THEY ARE MAKING SOME LAST TRADES BEFORE BATTLE.
THEY WANT HORSES.
THEY CAN'T HAVE BILLY!
I WOULDN'T TRADE FOR BILLY! NOT EVER!
ME NEITHER.

CHAPTER 5
NIGHT OF JUNE 28, 1846-- INSIDE FORT LARAMIE
...AND THAT'S HOW I BECAME THE FIRST WHITE MAN TO CIRCUMNAVIGATE THE GREAT SALT LAKE!
CLINK
WHAT AN ADVENTURE! YOU MUST KNOW THIS COUNTRY LIKE THE BACK OF YOUR HAND!
SURE DO!
JUST HOW GREAT IS THIS HASTINGS CUTOFF?
WHOA! NOT GOOD AT ALL! I JUST CAME THROUGH THERE A MONTH OR TWO AGO.
YOU'VE TAKEN THE SHORTCUT!?
SURE I DID. TOOK IT WITH LANSFORD HASTINGS HIMSELF.
YOU TOOK THE HASTINGS CUTOFF WITH MR. HASTINGS?!
TRUST ME, IT'S NO CUTOFF. HASTINGS IS A LAWYER-- HE'S NO TRAILBUSTER.
BUT HE'S WRITTEN UP THE SHORTCUT IN THIS BOOK!
I DON'T CARE WHAT THAT SILLY BOOK SAYS! I JUST CAME THROUGH THAT "SHORTCUT"! IT'S STEEP HILLS, CRAGGY MOUNTAINS, AND THICKETS, THEN YOU GET TO THE SALT LAKE DESERT--THE MOST DESOLATE COUNTRY ON THE GLOBE!
WHAM
I BARELY MADE IT THROUGH WITH MULES! NO WAGON'S GOING TO MAKE THAT JOURNEY!
BUT THE BOOK SAYS--
FORGET THE BOOK!
YOU TAKE THE REGULAR WAGON TRACK AND NEVER LEAVE IT!
IT'S BARELY POSSIBLE TO GET THROUGH IF YOU FOLLOW IT, AND IT MAY BE IMPOSSIBLE IF YOU DON'T! THINK OF YOUR FAMILY!
THANK YOU FOR YOUR ADVICE, LIEUTENANT.
IS HE LISTENING TO THAT GUY?
I WOULD LISTEN TO THAT GUY.
WE'LL FIND OUT SOON ENOUGH.

STUBBORN AS A MULE! I WARNED HIM! YOU CAN'T SAY I DIDN'T WARN HIM.
DID YOU TELL HIM THAT HASTINGS IS OUT THERE NOW, TAKING FOLKS THROUGH?
NO! AND DON'T YOU TELL HIM! THAT BLASTED LAWYER AND HIS SHORTCUT ARE GOING TO GET PEOPLE KILLED!
THAT'S A SHORTCUT TO DEATH, THAT'S ALL IT IS.
REST UP, GANG! WE'RE BACK ON THE ROAD TOMORROW! WE'VE GOT TO MAKE IT TO INDEPENDENCE ROCK BY INDEPENDENCE DAY!
THAT'S OVER 130 MILES IN LESS THAN A WEEK! BUT I'M SURE WE'LL MAKE IT!
JULY 4, 1846 INDEPENDENCE DAY, PLATTE RIVER
IS THIS INDEPENDENCE ROCK?
OF COURSE NOT!
WE'RE CLOSE ENOUGH, THOUGH. NOW, WHERE'S MY SPECIAL FOURTH OF JULY BOTTLE?
THIS ONE?
AT HIGH NOON, I SHALL FACE HOMEWARD AND TOAST OUR OLD FRIENDS IN SPRINGFIELD.
OLDE BRANDY
WHICH WAY IS DEAR OLD SPRINGFIELD?
IT'S EAST, POPPA, THAT WAY.
AH, YES. THAT WAY, INDEED!
CAN WE DRINK FROM THE SPECIAL BOTTLE?
GOOD HEAVENS, NO! THIS ISN'T FOR YOU!
POP
OLDE BRANDY
YOU MAY DRINK LEMONADE-- WE'VE GOT SOME DRIED LEMONS!
EVERYONE DRINK UP! IT'S THE FOURTH OF JULY!
HAPPY 70TH BIRTHDAY, AMERICA!

JULY 6, 1846
PLATTE RIVER
MORE SIOUX! LOOK AT ALL OF THEM!
THEY'RE ON THE *WARPATH*!
SSSSSSH! THE SIOUX COULD SLAUGHTER US *ALL*!
GRANDMA'S STORIES HAVE MADE YOU CHICKEN! THEY WANT TO FIGHT THE CROWS, NOT US.
THEY ARE THROWING STICKS.
GREEN TWIGS. THAT'S THE SIGN OF FRIENDSHIP.
OH NO! WHAT IF THEY *PONY-NAP* BILLY?!?
WHO'S THE CHICKEN, NOW?
GOODNESS! LOOK AT THEM! A TRUE FORCE TO BE RECKONED WITH!
DO WE GET TO SEE THEM FIGHT THE CROWS?
THE SIOUX WERE PRIMED FOR WAR. BUT NO MAJOR SIOUX CONFLICTS ARE RECORDED FROM THIS PERIOD.
UH-OH, VIRGINIA, THEY'RE COMING FOR BILLY!
EEEEEP!
LOOK, A MIRROR. LET ME CHECK MY WAR PAINT.
BWAAAAAGH!
HI-YAAA!
HEE-HEE! HA-HA!
DID YOU SEE THAT? I SCARED THEM OFF!
WITH A TELESCOPE!
THAT BIG WAGON HAS A MIRROR.
YEAH, YOU SHOULD CHECK YOUR PAINT.
YAAAAGH!
HA-HA-HA! SHE DID IT AGAIN!

JULY 12, 1846
INDEPENDENCE ROCK
THERE IT IS CHILDREN, INDEPENDENCE ROCK!
I'M GOING TO CARVE MY NAME!
CAN WE WRITE OUR NAMES?
YES! WE MUST ALL WRITE OUR NAMES!
THIS IS A RECORD OF MANY WHO PASSED THIS WAY. ISN'T IT GREAT?
WEREN'T WE SUPPOSED TO BE HERE A WEEK AGO?
WHAT'S A WEEK? WE'RE RIGHT ON TRACK--ESPECIALLY IF WE TAKE THE SHORTCUT!
LET'S SPEND THE WHOLE DAY HERE! WE HAVE ALL THE TIME IN THE WORLD!
JAmes Reed 1846
Virginia
PATTY REED 1846
1844
JULY 14, 1846
SOUTH PASS
WHAT'S THE COMMOTION? WHY ARE WE STOPPING?
PROVIDENCE! I KNEW IT!
A LETTER FROM LANSFORD HASTINGS HIMSELF!
LANSFORD HASTINGS IS HERE! HE'S GUIDING A GROUP THROUGH HIS SHORTCUT!
THE MAN HIMSELF! HE'S LEAVING FROM FORT BRIDGER!
SHOW THEM THE LETTER, MR. BONNEY!
HERE IT IS. MR. HASTINGS SAID I WAS TO SHOW IT TO TRAVELERS ON THE ROAD.
HA-HA! YOU HAVE SAVED US 300 MILES, MY GOOD MAN!
HA-HA! SHORTCUT! SHORTCUT! SHORTCUT!
I SURE HOPE THIS HASTINGS FELLOW KNOWS WHAT HE'S DOING.
ME TOO.

CHAPTER 6
JULY 20, 1846 - THE PARTING OF THE WAYS
INDEPENDENCE ROCK
FORT LARAMIE
SOUTH PASS
CHIMNEY ROCK
FORT BRIDGER
INDEPENDENCE
ARE THEY LEAVING WITHOUT US?
NOPE! WE ARE LEAVING THEM! THIS IS IT, THE SHORTCUT. AND THESE ARE THE BRAVE SOULS WHO WILL TRAVEL THROUGH IT!
WE'LL CAMP HERE TONIGHT AND CHOOSE A CAPTAIN FOR THE EXPEDITION.
AND I THINK I KNOW WHO IT WILL BE!
WHO?
WHO DO YOU THINK?
MR. DONNER?
PATRICK BREEN?
THAT GERMAN GUY?
NO! SOMEONE YOU ARE RELATED TO--
MOM?
THAT NIGHT
THE CANDIDATES FOR CAPTAIN ARE MR. GEORGE DONNER AND MYSELF.
I SHALL READ THE VOTES ALOUD.
DONNER!
HAH! THERE'S ONE FOR YOU, GEORGE.
DONNER.
HMPH. YOU ARE POPULAR, GEORGE.
DONNER, DONNER, DONNER, DONNER, GEORGE DONNER, REED!
THERE YOU ARE!
DONNER, DONNER, DONNER--BLAST! WE'LL BE CO-CAPTAINS!
WE SHALL BE CALLED THE REED-DONNER PARTY!
HOW ABOUT THE DONNOR-REED PARTY?
I DID WIN THE VOTE...
DONNER PARTY IT IS!
CONGRATULATIONS, GEORGE!
GRRRR.
HOW ARE WE RELATED TO GEORGE DONNER?

MEANWHILE AT FORT BRIDGER
WHY DO YOU PICK YOUR TEETH WITH THAT THING? IT'S DISGUSTING!
AIN'T DISGUSTIN'-- IT'S MY LUCKY ARROWHEAD.
WHAT MAKES IT SO LUCKY?
I CARRIED THIS IN MY HIP FOR FIVE YEARS.
IN YOUR POCKET?
NO, IN MY HIP.
I MADE THE MISTAKE OF COCKING MY GUN IN THE PRESENCE OF A BLACKFOOT CHIEF.
OOPS.
HAD TWO ARROWS IN ME 'FORE I HIT THE GROUND.
BLACKFOOT CHIEF TOOK MY RIFLE AND RODE AWAY ON MY PONY.
SHOULD'NA COCKED YOUR GUN.
WHO ARE THESE GUYS?
JIM BRIDGER AND LOUIS VASQUEZ. THEY ARE TRAPPERS. THEY TRAP AND SELL BEAVER PELTS.
THEY RUN FORT BRIDGER, A TRADING POST THE DONNER PARTY WILL SOON VISIT.
HAD A MISSIONARY FELLA CUT IT OUT OF ME.
HE HAD TO DIG DEEP.
SEE, IT WAS STUCK RIGHT IN THE BONE. THE BONE HAD GROWN RIGHT AROUND IT.
MUST'A HURT.
SURE DID.
AND NOW YOU PICK YOUR TEETH WITH IT.
AIN'T MUCH ELSE TO DO 'ROUND HERE.
NOBODY COMES THIS WAY.
WE SHOULD'A BUILT CLOSER TO THE MAIN ROUTE.
HERE COMES SOMEBODY!

IT'S A MULE TEAM.
TELL US THE TRUTH ABOUT THIS SHORTCUT. WE'VE HEARD IT'S A HARD STRETCH OF COUNTRY.
YEAH, BUT DISTANCE-WISE IT IS SHORTER.
YOUR MULES WILL MAKE THE TRIP JUST FINE--ESPECIALLY IF YOU AIN'T PULLIN' WAGONS.
THERE'S ANOTHER GROUP HEADED THIS WAY AND THEY DO HAVE WAGONS. FAMILIES IN WAGONS. GIVE THEM THIS LETTER WILL YOU?
GIVE IT TO VASQUEZ. I CAN'T EVEN READ MY OWN NAME. I'M PERFECTLY IGNORANT OF ALL KNOWLEDGE CONTAINED IN BOOKS.
SEE THAT THEY GET THIS LETTER. IT'S VERY IMPORTANT!
WE'LL PASS IT ALONG.
WHAT'S THIS IMPORTANT LETTER SAY?
IT SAYS,
TO JAMES REED, GEORGE DONNER, AND CO.
AVOID THIS CUTOFF! THERE IS NO WATER, LITTLE FEED, AND MANY HAZARDS! RETURN TO THE MAIN ROAD FOR YOUR FAMILY'S SAFETY!
BE SAFE, TURN AROUND NOW!
YOUR FRIEND, EDWIN BRYANT
HMM.
WE'VE GOT A BIG GROUP COMING IN, DO WE?
HASTINGS MAY BE AN IDIOT, BUT HE IS BRINGING TRAFFIC OUR WAY.
WHO KNOWS, MAYBE WITH ENOUGH TRAFFIC, THE ROUTE WILL GET BETTER.
MORE TRAFFIC... MORE BUSINESS FOR US.
YOU KEEP THAT LETTER SAFE, VASQUEZ.
I SURELY WILL.

JULY 22, 1846
THE ROAD TO FORT BRIDGER
POPPA, BILLY'S ACTING FUNNY.
THAT ANIMAL IS NOT WELL.
POOR BILLY!
THE OXEN ARE ACTING FUNNY TOO.
I THINK THIS WATER MAY BE POISONING THE ANIMALS.
AND IT TASTES HORRIBLE!
DON'T DRINK THAT WATER, JAMES!
PTEWW!
THE WATER WAS POISON, FILLED WITH ALKALI.
WHUMP
OH NO! BERTHA!

JULY 26, 1846 FORT BRIDGER
...AND THAT'S WHEN I DISCOVERED THE PETRIFIED FOREST. WITH PETRIFIED BIRDS A SINGIN' IN THE BRANCHES.
HUH? JIM, ALL YOUR STORIES ARE CRAZY.
CALL ME BY MY CROW NAME: CASAPY, CHIEF OF BLANKETS. WANNA HEAR HOW I GOT THAT NAME?
YOU TOLD ME THAT ONE ALREADY. HEY, HERE COMES THAT WAGON PARTY.
TIME TO PLAY HOST.
WELCOME, WEARY TRAVELERS. REST YOUR BONES!
I AM CAPTAIN GEORGE DONNER AND THIS IS--
WHERE IS LANSFORD HASTINGS? IS HE STILL HERE?
MR. HASTINGS AND HIS CREW LEFT SEVERAL DAYS AGO, BUT YOU SHOULD BE ABLE TO CATCH THEM.
WE LOST MANY OXEN ON THE WAY HERE--POISON WATER.
WE HAVE FRESH ANIMALS HERE, AT A FAIR PRICE.
I DOUBT THAT! THE TRADERS WE'VE MET ARE AS GREAT A SET OF SHARKS AS EVER DISGRACED HUMANITY!
HAH! YOU'LL FIND NO SHARKS HERE. WE'LL SELL YOU ALL YOU NEED AT A FAIR PRICE.
TAKE YOUR REST.
THEN YOU CAN CATCH UP WITH MR. HASTINGS.
HOW IS THE TRAIL? WE'VE HEARD MANY DIFFERENT REPORTS.
THE HASTINGS CUTOFF IS A FINE, LEVEL ROAD, WITH PLENTY OF WATER AND GRASS--THERE IS A SMALL, FORTY-MILE STRETCH WITH NO WATER. OTHER THAN THAT, IT'S PARADISE!
WONDERFUL! YOU ARE EXCELLENT AND ACCOMMODATING GENTLEMEN!
HEAR THAT, VASQUEZ? "EXCELLENT AND ACCOMMODATING GENTLEMEN."
NO SHARKS HERE.
THOSE DIRTY DEALERS! WHY DIDN'T THEY SHOW THEM THAT LETTER?
WE CAN ONLY WONDER. MAYBE THEY WERE GREEDY, MAYBE THEY FORGOT. IN ANY CASE, DO YOU THINK THAT LETTER WOULD HAVE CHANGED JAMES REED'S MIND?
I DOUBT IT.
SO DO I.

CHAPTER 7
AUGUST 2, 1846 HASTINGS CUTOFF
HA-HA! IT IS A PARADISE!
I LOVE IT--NO DUST! WE'VE EATEN WAGON TRAIN DUST FOR THE LAST TIME! WE'LL MAKE IT TO CALIFORNIA IN AN EASY SEVEN WEEKS!
WE'RE THE LUCKIEST EMIGRANTS ON THE TRAIL!
WATCH, POPPA! I'M RACING EDDY BREEN!
HA! SHOW HIM WHO'S BEST!
WHO IS EDDY BREEN?
THE BREENS ARE AN IRISH FAMILY; THREE WAGONS AND SEVEN KIDS. THEY HAVE RECENTLY JOINED THE DONNER PARTY.
HOLD ON. THAT'S NOT BILLY! WHERE IS BILLY THE PONY?
DON'T WORRY ABOUT BILLY THE PONY.
WHY? WHAT HAPPEND TO BILLY?
ARE YOU SURE YOU WANT TO HEAR THIS?
HEAR WHAT?
BILLY WAS SET LOOSE. HE WAS TOO WORN OUT TO TRAVEL ANY FARTHER.
THAT PONY WAS DEAD ON HIS FEET.
NO HE WASN'T. I'M SURE HE WENT AND FOUND A NICE MEADOW TO LIVE IN. RIGHT?
WHO KNOWS. MAYBE.
YES. THAT'S WHAT HAPPENS!
BILLY MOST LIKELY ENDED UP AS DINNER FOR SOMEONE FARTHER DOWN THE WAGON TRAIN.
FRESH MEAT WOULDN'T BE WASTED.

NOOOOOOOO!!

I'M WINNING!
I'M WINNING!
NO YOU AREN'T! I'LL WIN FOR--
AAAAAAAAAAAAAAAAAAAAGH
CRUNCH
OH NO! HIS LEG IS BROKEN!
OH, EDDY!
WE'LL HAVE TO GO BACK TO FORT BRIDGER!
IS THERE A DOCTOR AT THE FORT?
I'M A SURGEON!
THANK YOU, GOOD SIR!
YUP. IT'LL HAVE TO COME OFF.
THE BOOT?
NOPE. THE WHOLE LEG.
AAAAAAAAGH! DON'T CUT IT! DON'T CUT IT!
WE'LL TAKE OUR CHANCES WITH A SPLINT.
AWW. NOBODY EVER LET'S ME OPERATE.
C'MON, SAW, LET'S GO BACK TO CUTTIN' DOWN TREES.

AUGUST 7, 1846
MOUTH OF WEBER CANYON
I SAY, WHAT'S THIS?
IT'S A NOTE-- FROM LANSFORD HASTINGS!
GIVE IT HERE! WHAT DOES IT SAY?
IT SAYS, "STAY HERE, WAIT FOR MESSAGE. NEW ROUTE PLANNED."
WAIT HERE!? NEW ROUTE!? IT CAN'T SAY THAT!
IT DOES.
WE CAN'T JUST STAY HERE!
I DON'T WANT A NEW ROUTE! I WANT THIS ROUTE!
CALM DOWN-- YOU'VE TRUSTED HASTINGS THIS FAR.
HASTINGS IS SOMEWHERE IN THIS CANYON! I SAY WE GO FIND HIM!
WE SHOULD GO BACK TO THE MAIN ROAD!
IT'S ONLY SIX DAYS BEHIND US.
GO BACK? NONSENSE!
WE CAN'T WASTE TIME BACKTRACKING!
I'LL GO AND FIND HASTINGS MYSELF!!

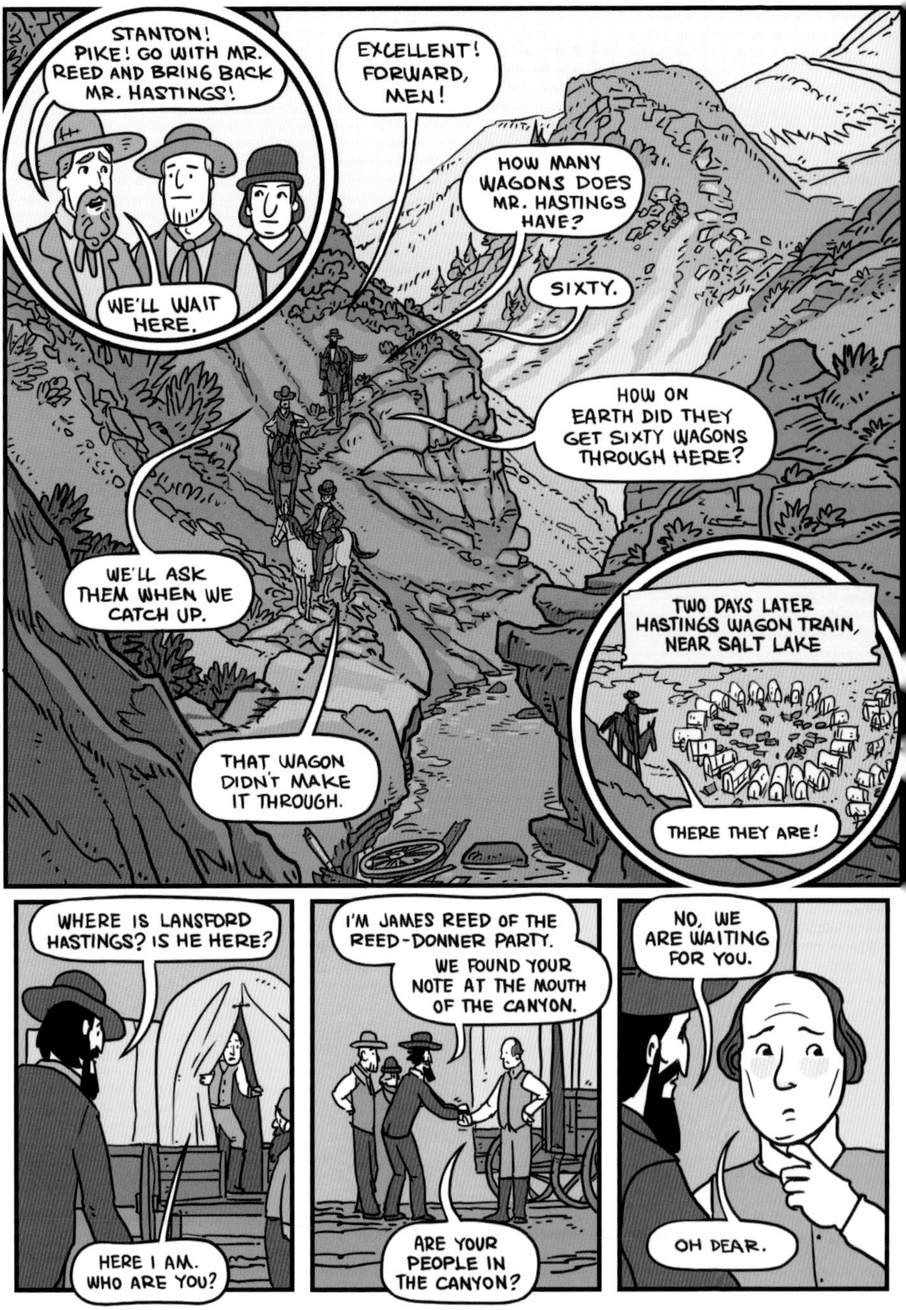
STANTON! PIKE! GO WITH MR. REED AND BRING BACK MR. HASTINGS!
WE'LL WAIT HERE.
EXCELLENT! FORWARD, MEN!
HOW MANY WAGONS DOES MR. HASTINGS HAVE?
SIXTY.
HOW ON EARTH DID THEY GET SIXTY WAGONS THROUGH HERE?
WE'LL ASK THEM WHEN WE CATCH UP.
THAT WAGON DIDN'T MAKE IT THROUGH.
TWO DAYS LATER
HASTINGS WAGON TRAIN, NEAR SALT LAKE
THERE THEY ARE!
WHERE IS LANSFORD HASTINGS? IS HE HERE?
HERE I AM. WHO ARE YOU?
I'M JAMES REED OF THE REED-DONNER PARTY.
WE FOUND YOUR NOTE AT THE MOUTH OF THE CANYON.
ARE YOUR PEOPLE IN THE CANYON?
NO, WE ARE WAITING FOR YOU.
OH DEAR.

THIS CANYON WAS A **MISTAKE.**
WHAT DO YOU MEAN?
WE HAD TO LOWER *ONE* WAGON AT A TIME--AND IT TOOK *EVERY* ANIMAL WE HAD.
WAGONS WAS DOIN' THINGS NO WAGON WAS MEANT TO DO!
I SAW AN OX AND WAGON FALL A HUNDRED FEET.
IT'S NOT **MY** FAULT--THE ADVANCE PARTY TOOK THE WRONG ROUTE.
CAN YOU SHOW US THE CORRECT ROUTE?
YES, I SUPPOSE I CAN.
SHOW ME THE WAY! I'LL NEED A FRESH HORSE!
PIKE, STANTON, I'LL SEE YOU BACK AT CAMP.
MR. HASTINGS, LEAD THE WAY!
FOLLOW ME.
LATER
MOUTH OF WEBER CANYON
HERE COME PIKE AND STANTON!
FINALLY! WHERE IS REED?
HE'S NOT BACK YET?
WE HAVEN'T SEEN HIM.
HE WAS HEADED THIS WAY WITH MR. HASTINGS.
HE LOST OUR ***GUIDE?***

LOOK, MR. REED, I'VE GOT TO GET BACK TO MY WAGONS ARE **YOU** A GOOD GUIDE?
CERTAINLY!
THE ROUTE I PLANNED WAS ***NOT*** THIS CANYON.
WELL, WHERE ***WAS*** YOUR ROUTE?
IT'S... OVER ***THAT*** WAY.
ANYTHING MORE SPECIFIC THAN THAT?
NOPE. THE PLANNED ROUTE WAS THAT WAY. ***ANY*** ROUTE WILL BE BETTER THAN THIS CANYON.
THAT WAY?
THAT WAY. WE SHALL MEET AGAIN IN THE SALT LAKE VALLEY.
SEE YOU THERE.
DAYS LATER MOUTH OF WEBER CANYON
READY THE WAGONS! OUR ROUTE IS CLEAR!
WHERE HAVE YOU **BEEN**! WE'VE BEEN SEARCHING THE HILLS FOR YOU.
I HAVE BLAZED OUR TRAIL!
YOU KNOW THE ROUTE?
I ***DO***. I HAVE NAMED IT ***"REED'S GAP."***
I THINK *REED'S GAP* IS IN HIS BRAIN.

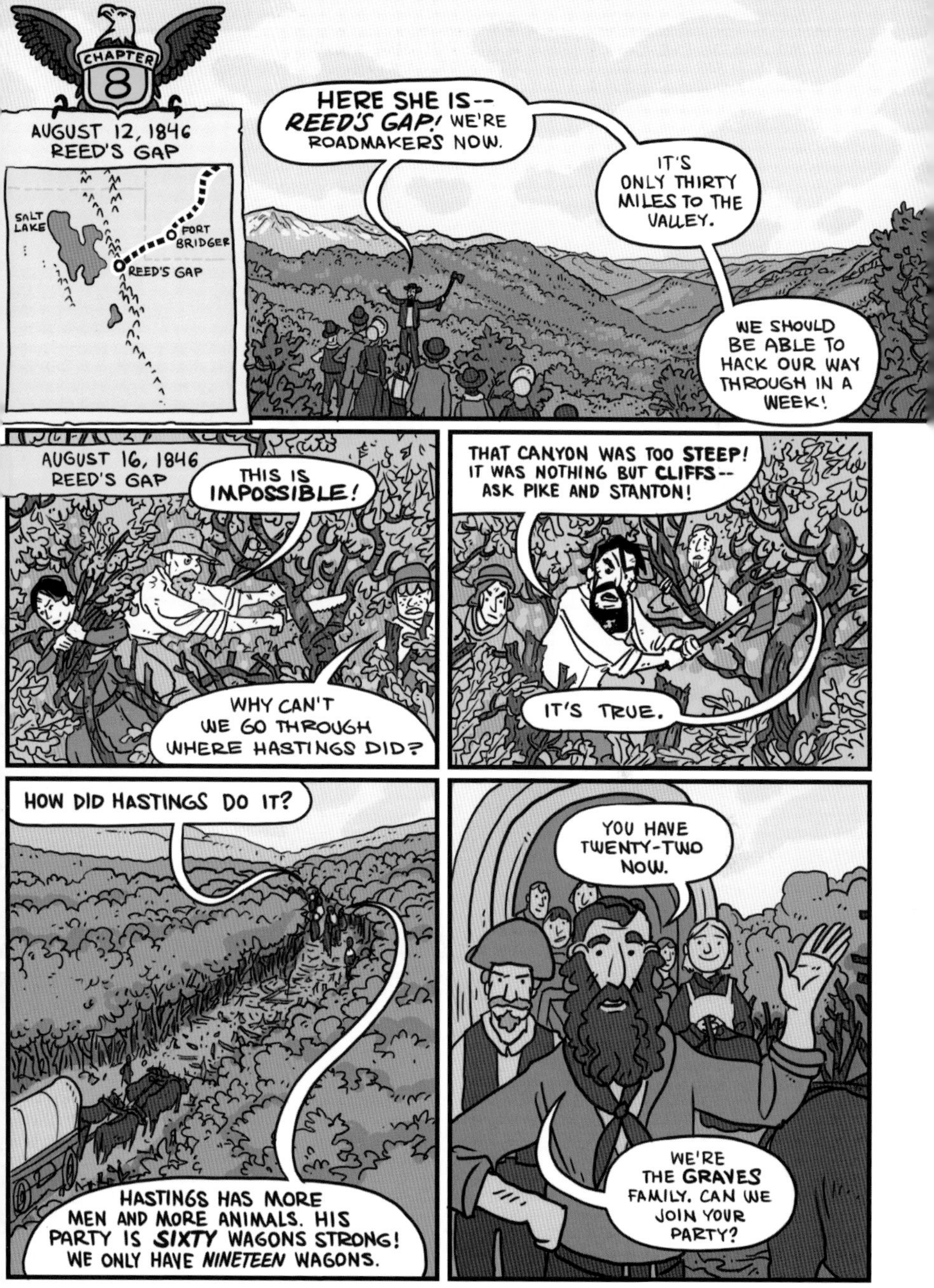
CHAPTER 8
AUGUST 12, 1846
REED'S GAP
SALT LAKE
FORT BRIDGER
REED'S GAP
HERE SHE IS-- *REED'S GAP!* WE'RE ROADMAKERS NOW.
IT'S ONLY THIRTY MILES TO THE VALLEY.
WE SHOULD BE ABLE TO HACK OUR WAY THROUGH IN A WEEK!
AUGUST 16, 1846
REED'S GAP
THIS IS **IMPOSSIBLE!**
WHY CAN'T WE GO THROUGH WHERE HASTINGS DID?
THAT CANYON WAS TOO **STEEP!** IT WAS NOTHING BUT **CLIFFS**-- ASK PIKE AND STANTON!
IT'S TRUE.
HOW DID HASTINGS DO IT?
HASTINGS HAS MORE MEN AND MORE ANIMALS. HIS PARTY IS ***SIXTY*** WAGONS STRONG! WE ONLY HAVE *NINETEEN* WAGONS.
YOU HAVE TWENTY-TWO NOW.
WE'RE THE **GRAVES** FAMILY. CAN WE JOIN YOUR PARTY?

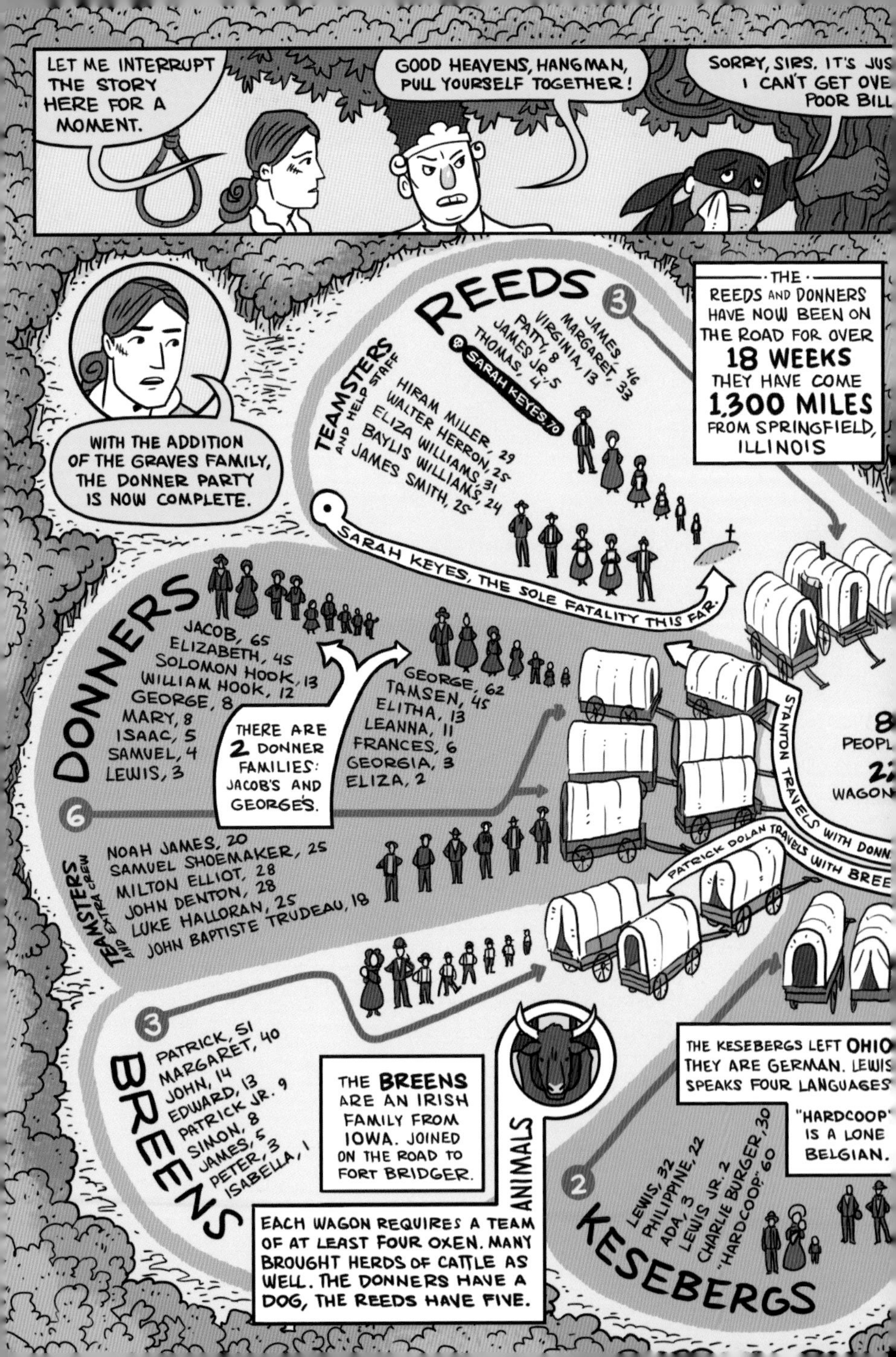

LET ME INTERRUPT THE STORY HERE FOR A MOMENT.
GOOD HEAVENS, HANGMAN, PULL YOURSELF TOGETHER!
SORRY, SIRS. IT'S JUS I CAN'T GET OVE POOR BILL
WITH THE ADDITION OF THE GRAVES FAMILY, THE DONNER PARTY IS NOW COMPLETE.
THE REEDS AND DONNERS HAVE NOW BEEN ON THE ROAD FOR OVER 18 WEEKS THEY HAVE COME 1,300 MILES FROM SPRINGFIELD, ILLINOIS
REEDS
3
JAMES, 46
MARGARET, 33
VIRGINIA, 13
PATTY, 8
JAMES JR., 5
THOMAS, 4
SARAH KEYES, 70
TEAMSTERS AND HELP STAFF
HIRAM MILLER, 29
WALTER HERRON, 25
ELIZA WILLIAMS, 31
BAYLIS WILLIAMS, 24
JAMES SMITH, 25
SARAH KEYES, THE SOLE FATALITY THIS FAR.
DONNERS
6
JACOB, 65
ELIZABETH, 45
SOLOMON HOOK, 13
WILLIAM HOOK, 12
GEORGE, 8
MARY, 8
ISAAC, 5
SAMUEL, 4
LEWIS, 3
THERE ARE 2 DONNER FAMILIES: JACOB'S AND GEORGE'S.
GEORGE, 62
TAMSEN, 45
ELITHA, 13
LEANNA, 11
FRANCES, 6
GEORGIA, 3
ELIZA, 2
TEAMSTERS AND EXTRA CREW
NOAH JAMES, 20
SAMUEL SHOEMAKER, 25
MILTON ELLIOT, 28
JOHN DENTON, 28
LUKE HALLORAN, 25
JOHN BAPTISTE TRUDEAU, 18
STANTON TRAVELS WITH DONN
PATRICK DOLAN TRAVELS WITH BREE
PEOPL
WAGON
3
BREENS
PATRICK, 51
MARGARET, 40
JOHN, 14
EDWARD, 13
PATRICK JR. 9
SIMON, 8
JAMES, 5
PETER, 3
ISABELLA, 1
THE BREENS ARE AN IRISH FAMILY FROM IOWA. JOINED ON THE ROAD TO FORT BRIDGER.
ANIMALS
EACH WAGON REQUIRES A TEAM OF AT LEAST FOUR OXEN. MANY BROUGHT HERDS OF CATTLE AS WELL. THE DONNERS HAVE A DOG, THE REEDS HAVE FIVE.
THE KESEBERGS LEFT OHIO THEY ARE GERMAN. LEWIS SPEAKS FOUR LANGUAGES
"HARDCOOP" IS A LONE BELGIAN.
2
KESEBERGS
LEWIS, 32
PHILIPPINE, 22
ADA, 3
LEWIS JR. 2
CHARLIE BURGER, 30
"HARDCOOP," 60

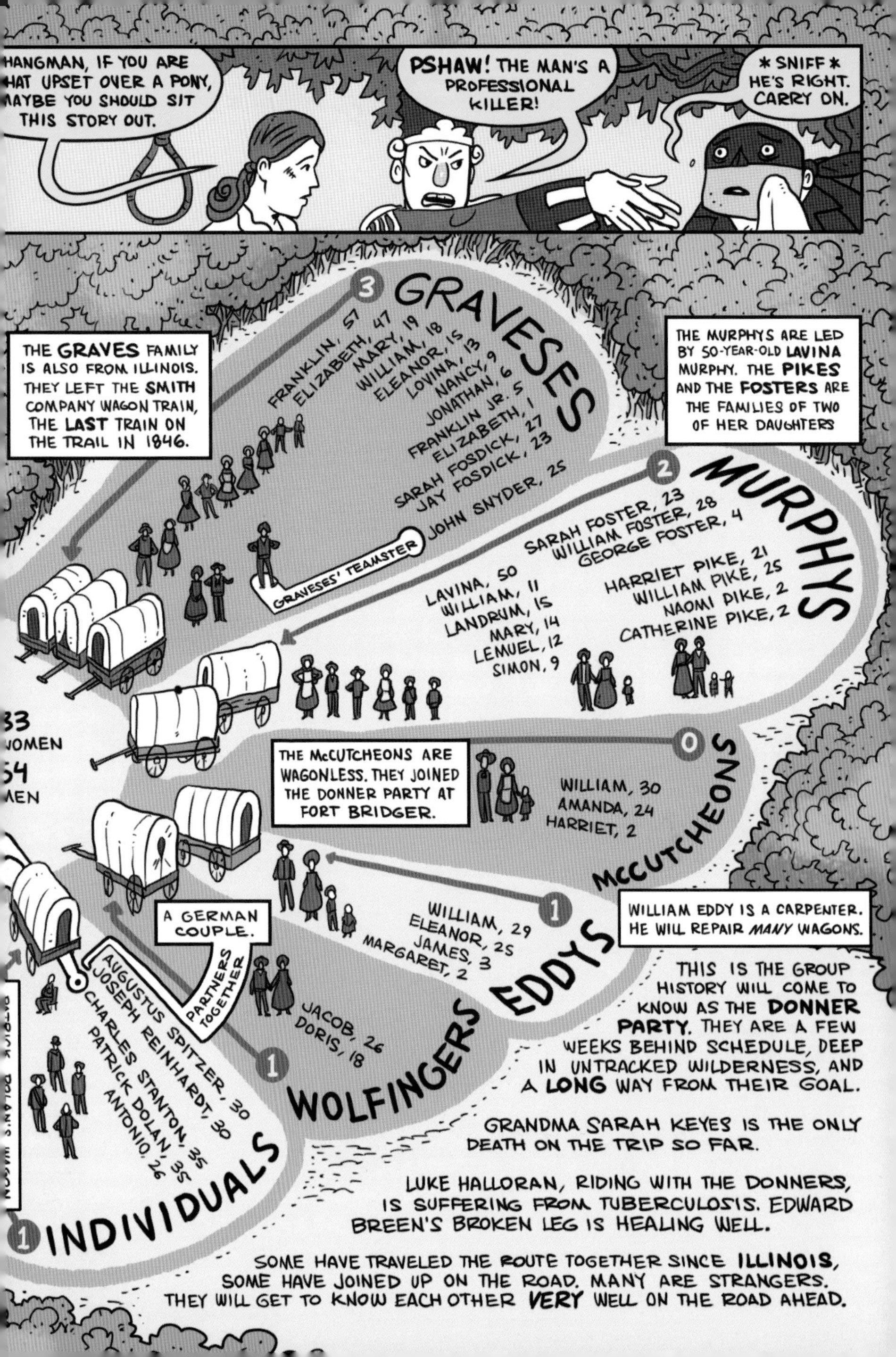

HANGMAN, IF YOU ARE HAT UPSET OVER A PONY, MAYBE YOU SHOULD SIT THIS STORY OUT.
PSHAW! THE MAN'S A PROFESSIONAL KILLER!
SNIFF HE'S RIGHT. CARRY ON.
THE GRAVES FAMILY IS ALSO FROM ILLINOIS. THEY LEFT THE SMITH COMPANY WAGON TRAIN, THE LAST TRAIN ON THE TRAIL IN 1846.
3 GRAVESES
FRANKLIN, 57
ELIZABETH, 47
MARY, 19
WILLIAM, 18
ELEANOR, 15
LOVINA, 13
NANCY, 9
JONATHAN, 6
FRANKLIN JR. 5
ELIZABETH, 1
SARAH FOSDICK, 23
JAY FOSDICK, 23
JOHN SNYDER, 25
GRAVESES' TEAMSTER
THE MURPHYS ARE LED BY 50-YEAR-OLD LAVINA MURPHY. THE PIKES AND THE FOSTERS ARE THE FAMILIES OF TWO OF HER DAUGHTERS
2 MURPHYS
SARAH FOSTER, 23
WILLIAM FOSTER, 28
GEORGE FOSTER, 4
LAVINA, 50
WILLIAM, 11
LANDRUM, 15
MARY, 14
LEMUEL, 12
SIMON, 9
HARRIET PIKE, 21
WILLIAM PIKE, 25
NAOMI PIKE, 2
CATHERINE PIKE, 2
33 WOMEN
54 MEN
THE McCUTCHEONS ARE WAGONLESS. THEY JOINED THE DONNER PARTY AT FORT BRIDGER.
0 McCUTCHEONS
WILLIAM, 30
AMANDA, 24
HARRIET, 2
1 EDDYS
WILLIAM, 29
ELEANOR, 25
JAMES, 3
MARGARET, 2
WILLIAM EDDY IS A CARPENTER. HE WILL REPAIR MANY WAGONS.
A GERMAN COUPLE.
1 WOLFINGERS
JACOB, 26
DORIS, 18
PARTNERS TOGETHER
1 INDIVIDUALS
AUGUSTUS SPITZER, 30
JOSEPH REINHARDT, 30
CHARLES STANTON, 35
PATRICK DOLAN, 35
ANTONIO, 26
PATRICK DOLAN'S WAGON
THIS IS THE GROUP HISTORY WILL COME TO KNOW AS THE DONNER PARTY. THEY ARE A FEW WEEKS BEHIND SCHEDULE, DEEP IN UNTRACKED WILDERNESS, AND A LONG WAY FROM THEIR GOAL.
GRANDMA SARAH KEYES IS THE ONLY DEATH ON THE TRIP SO FAR.
LUKE HALLORAN, RIDING WITH THE DONNERS, IS SUFFERING FROM TUBERCULOSIS. EDWARD BREEN'S BROKEN LEG IS HEALING WELL.
SOME HAVE TRAVELED THE ROUTE TOGETHER SINCE ILLINOIS, SOME HAVE JOINED UP ON THE ROAD. MANY ARE STRANGERS. THEY WILL GET TO KNOW EACH OTHER VERY WELL ON THE ROAD AHEAD.

AUGUST 18, 1846
REED'S GAP
ARE YOU SURE THIS IS THE ROUTE HASTINGS POINTED OUT?
CHOP
CHOP
CHOP
YES, I'M POSITIVE.
CHOP
CHOP
CHOP
THE HASTINGS PARTY WAS BIGGER. THEY COULD HAVE CHOPPED THROUGH IN A DAY OR TWO!
WHY SHOULD WE FOLLOW HASTINGS'S DIRECTIONS?
HE GOT LOST ON HIS OWN ROUTE!
CHOP
CHOP
IT DOESN'T MATTER ANYMORE. THIS IS THE ROUTE WE'RE ON!
GET CHOPPING!
AUGUST 20, 1846
REED'S GAP
I HATE REED'S GAP.
WE ALL HATE REED'S GAP!
YOU'RE LUCKY YOU BROKE THAT LEG, EDDY.
LAZY DAYS. I LOVE REED'S GAP!
WHAP
NEVER PRAISE LAZINESS, EDWARD. OR I'LL GO FIND THAT SURGEON!
YIPE!

AUGUST 21, 1846
REED'S GAP
WE ARE ALMOST OUT!
THE RIVERBED AHEAD IS A DENSE WILLOW THICKET, THE HILL ABOVE IT IS A STEEP, HARD CLIMB.
CHOP OR CLIMB?
HILL!
HILL!
OVER THE HILL!
I CAN'T TAKE ANY MORE CHOPPING!
DOUBLE-TEAM THE WAGONS. IT'LL BE A BIG PULL.
MORE LIKE QUADRUPLE-TEAM!
LOOK AT THIS! IT'S TAKING EVERY ANIMAL WE'VE GOT TO PULL ONE WAGON!
WE'LL HAVE TO HAUL 'EM OVER ONE AT A TIME!
BEHOLD THE VALLEY OF THE GREAT SALT LAKE!
WE HAVE CROSSED THE WASATCH MOUNTAINS AT LAST!
AND IT ONLY TOOK MOST OF AUGUST.

ONE YEAR FROM NOW, IN 1847, A GROUP LEAD BY A MAN NAMED BRIGHAM YOUNG WILL LOOK OUT ON THIS SAME VALLEY AND CALL THEIR JOURNEY OVER.
IT IS ENOUGH.
THIS IS THE RIGHT PLACE.
BRIGHAM YOUNG AND HIS FOLLOWERS WILL BUILD A CITY IN THE SALT LAKE VALLEY.
BUT IN 1846, THE VALLEY IS A MARSH. HOME TO UTE, PAIUTE, GOSHUTE, AND SHOSHONE ENCAMPMENTS.
THE DONNER PARTY CROSSES THE VALLEY QUICKLY.
I'LL TAKE MARSHES OVER THICKETS ANY DAY!
SADLY, ONE MEMBER OF THE PARTY WILL DIE HERE.
OH NO! NOT YOUNG EDDY BREEN!
GANGRENE. I KNEW IT!
HE SHOULD HAVE LET THAT SURGEON AMPUTATE!
NO. EDDY IS FINE.
LUKE HALLORAN DIES OF TUBERCULOSIS.
WHO?
LUKE HALLORAN JOINED THE DONNERS AT FORT BRIDGER.
HE WAS VERY SICK.
THE DONNER PARTY DEATH TOLL IS NOW TWO. GRANDMA KEYES AND LUKE HALLORAN.
AND BILLY THE PONY, I GUESS.
UH-UH! BILLY LIVES!

AUGUST 28, 1846
HOPE WELLS
LOOK! TINY PAPERS!
IT'S ANOTHER NOTE FROM HASTINGS!
LOOKS LIKE THE BIRDS ATE IT.
CURSE YOU, BIRDS!
HOW WILL WE GET HASTINGS'S HELP NOW?
I'VE HAD JUST ABOUT ENOUGH OF HASTINGS'S HELP.
GATHER UP THE PIECES, CHILDREN. WE'LL MAKE A PUZZLE OF IT.
HERE'S SOME!
I'VE GOT ONE!
HERE'S MORE!
LET'S SEE WHAT IT SAYS.
TWO DAYS
TWO NIGHTS
HARD DRIVING
CROSS
DESERT
REACH WATER
THIS MUST BE THE FORTY-MILE DRY STRETCH JIM BRIDGER MENTIONED.
JIM BRIDGER?! THE MAN WHO SAID THIS SHORTCUT WAS "A FLAT ROAD TO PARADISE"?! THAT JIM BRIDGER?!
TWO DAYS' AND NIGHTS' HARD DRIVING? THAT SOUNDS A PIECE FARTHER THAN FORTY MILES.
WELL, WE HAVE NO CHOICE NOW.
WE MUST CROSS THE DESERT.

AUGUST 29, 1846
HASTINGS PASS
THE OXEN ARE IN NO SHAPE TO CROSS THAT!
WE'VE RESTED AS LONG AS WE CAN. IT'S TIME TO GO.
PACK AS MUCH WATER AS YOU CAN.
FILL EVERY BARREL.
HOLD ON. THE MORE WATER THEY LOAD,
THE HEAVIER THE WAGONS WILL BE,
AND THE THIRSTIER THE OXEN WILL GET.
IT'S A VICIOUS, VICIOUS CIRCLE.
WHAT CHOICE DO THEY HAVE?
THEY COULD JUST STAY THERE!
JOHN BREEN DID SAY, LATER, THAT THEY SHOULD HAVE SPENT THE WINTER THERE.
MY BETSY WILL DRINK TWENTY GALLONS A DAY.
I NEED A HUNDRED GALLONS A DAY FOR MY TEAM.
WE CAN HAUL THREE, MAYBE FOUR BARRELS.
THAT'S FORTY GALLONS TO LAST TWO DAYS.
TWO DAYS IF HASTINGS'S NOTE IS CORRECT...
AND I DOUBT THAT IT IS.

IS THIS THE DESERT?
IT MUST BE, BUT IT DOESN'T LOOK TOO DRY. THERE ARE *TREES*.
WE AIM FOR THAT PEAK.
AIN'T ***NO WAY*** THAT PEAK IS ONLY FORTY MILES AWAY.
NO MORE TREES-- BUT THERE'S BUSHES.
NO MORE BUSHES-- BUT THERE'S GRASS.
NO MORE GRASS.
NO MORE *ANYTHING*.

CHAPTER
9
AUGUST 30, 1846
SALT FLATS

I'M GLAD BILLY DIDN'T COME HERE. IT SEEMS AS THOUGH THE HAND OF DEATH HAS BEEN LAID UPON THIS COUNTRY.

WHAT A DESOLATE PLACE!
IT'S LIKE A FROZEN LAKE
BUT WITH NO WATER,
AND NOT FROZEN.
IT ACTUALLY IS AN ANCIENT DRY LAKE.
DURING THE ICE AGE, LAKE BONNEVILLE WAS ONE OF NORTH AMERICA'S LARGEST AND DEEPEST LAKES.
SALT LAKE
LAKE BONNEVILLE SHORELINE 20,000 B.C.
ALL THAT REMAINS NOW IS THE SALT LAKE AND THIS HARD SALT PAN.
FLAT AS A PAN, HUH?
THIS DESERT IS SO FLAT AND SO EMPTY, IN THE FUTURE IT WILL BE USED TO TEST LAND SPEED RECORDS.
WHAT IS THAT?
THIS IS A ROCKET CAR BUILT IN 1970.
AND HERE, AT THE BONNEVILLE SALT FLATS, IT WILL ACHIEVE A TOP SPEED OF 630 MILES AN HOUR...
WOW!
THE BLUE FLAME
A WORLD SPEED RECORD THAT WILL LAST 27 YEARS.
MUST HAVE TAKEN A LOT OF OXEN TO GO THAT FAST.
IF THE DONNER PARTY HAD THAT--THEY'D GET TO CALIFORNIA IN A DAY!

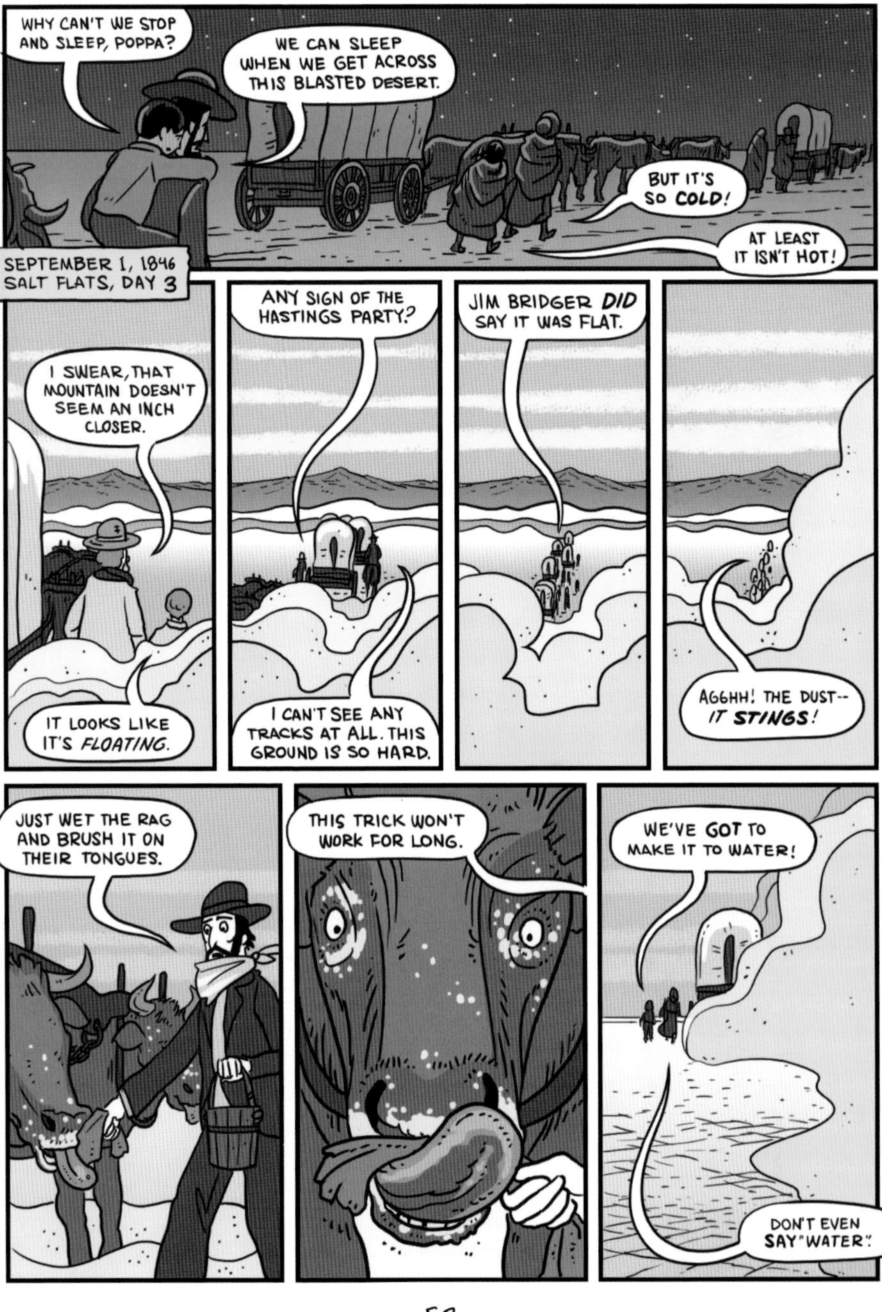
WHY CAN'T WE STOP AND SLEEP, POPPA?
WE CAN SLEEP WHEN WE GET ACROSS THIS BLASTED DESERT.
BUT IT'S SO COLD!
AT LEAST IT ISN'T HOT!
SEPTEMBER 1, 1846 SALT FLATS, DAY 3
I SWEAR, THAT MOUNTAIN DOESN'T SEEM AN INCH CLOSER.
IT LOOKS LIKE IT'S FLOATING.
ANY SIGN OF THE HASTINGS PARTY?
I CAN'T SEE ANY TRACKS AT ALL. THIS GROUND IS SO HARD.
JIM BRIDGER DID SAY IT WAS FLAT.
AGGHH! THE DUST-- IT STINGS!
JUST WET THE RAG AND BRUSH IT ON THEIR TONGUES.
THIS TRICK WON'T WORK FOR LONG.
WE'VE GOT TO MAKE IT TO WATER!
DON'T EVEN SAY "WATER".

SEPTEMBER 2, 1846
SALT FLATS, DAY 4
MUD!? HOW CAN THERE BE MUD IF THERE'S NO WATER?
WHY DID WE EVER LEAVE SPRINGFIELD?

CALIFORNIA CAN'T POSSIBLY BE WORTH THIS MUCH TROUBLE!
WE AREN'T PUSHING FOR CALIFORNIA NOW--
WE'RE PUSHING TO STAY ALIVE.

ENOUGH OF THIS!
I'M GOING TO RIDE AHEAD AND FIND WATER!
UNHITCH MY TEAMS. I WON'T HAVE THEM TAKE ANOTHER STEP WITHOUT WATER.
THEY MIGHT BOLT-- THEY'RE HALF MAD WITH THIRST.
THEY JUST NEED WATER! AND I'M GOING TO GO FIND SOME.
NOW UNHITCH THEM!
DADDY'S ALWAYS RIDING OFF TO SAVE US.
I HOPE HE CAN SAVE US THIS TIME.
MOMMA, CAN I SLEEP NOW?
WE SHOULD PROBABLY ALL SLEEP WHILE WE CAN.
CATCH 'EM! CATCH 'EM!
IS IT A STAMPEDE?
IT'S THE OXEN--THEY RAN AWAY!

SEPTEMBER 3, 1846
SALT FLATS, DAY 5
I FOUND WATER!
THERE'S A SMALL SPRING AT THE BASE OF THAT PEAK.
WHERE ARE THE OXEN?
THEY RAN AWAY.
WHY DID YOU UNHITCH THEM!?
YOU TOLD US TO!
YOU DID.
BLAST!
HOW WILL WE PULL THE WAGONS?
WE'LL GO AHEAD TO THE SPRING ON FOOT,
THEN FIND THE ANIMALS,
THEN COME BACK HERE FOR THE WAGONS.
WE'RE LEAVING THE WAGONS?
YES!!
YES,
BUT WE'RE COMING BACK FOR THEM!
I'LL GO ANYWHERE THERE'S WATER.
EVERYBODY UP-- WE'VE GOT MILES TO WALK.

THE KIDS CAN'T GO ANY FARTHER. WE'VE GOT TO STOP AND REST!
KEEP WALKING. WE *MUST* REACH THAT SPRING BEFORE THE SUN COMES UP.
THERE ARE THE DONNERS. CAN WE REST WITH THEM?
THEY'RE ASLEEP.
WE'LL SLEEP TOO, UNDER THE WAGON.
YIP!
YAP!
YIP!
WHAT?
WHATZAT?
SOMETHING IS OUT THERE.
IT'S *BIG!*
YAP!
YAP!
YIP!
IT'S A *MONSTER!*
STAY DOWN, CHILDREN!
YAP!
YIP!
HUH?
KIDS--IT'S ONE OF OUR CATTLE!
THEY'RE COMING BACK!
C'MERE, GIRL.
ONLY A COW.
NOT A MONSTER?
WE'RE ALL AWAKE NOW, LET'S KEEP MOVING.

SEPTEMBER 6, 1846 THE SPRING
WE MADE IT! WE'RE THE LAST ONES, BUT WE MADE IT!
FORTY MILES? FORTY MILES? THAT WAS EIGHTY MILES OF DESERT!
WE CAN REST ONE DAY, THEN WE HAVE TO MOVE.
THAT SHOULD GIVE ME TIME TO FIND MY ANIMALS AND RETRIEVE MY WAGONS.
YOU MIGHT HAFTA LEAVE A WAGON BEHIND. WE DID.
SO DID WE.
NONSENSE! I'M NOT LEAVING ANYTHING IN THIS GODFORSAKEN PLACE!
I HAVE NINE YOKE OF CATTLE.
THEY CAN'T ALL BE LOST!
TWO DAYS LATER...
THEY ARE ALL LOST!
IT MUST BE INDIANS! INDIANS STOLE MY CATTLE!
CALM DOWN, REED!
CALM DOWN!? HOW AM I SUPPOSED TO HAUL MY WAGONS --WITH MY DOGS!?
WE CAN LOAN YOU OXEN.
FOR THREE WAGONS?!!
FOR...ONE WAGON.

EVERYTHING **MUST** FIT INTO ONE WAGON.
TAKE ONLY THE NECESSITIES.
WHAT ABOUT MY DOLLS?
CAN YOU **EAT** THEM?
NO.
THEN *NO DOLLS.*
CURSE THIS DESERT.
WHEN WE ENTERED IT, WE WERE THE WEALTHIEST FAMILY IN THE PARTY.
NOW WE'RE THE POOREST.
REED! YOU WILL SLOW THE PARTY WITH THAT SETUP!
I'M SURE WE'LL BE **FINE**!
HUSH, JAMES.
PLEASE, MR. REED, TAKE TWO YOKE OF MY OXEN. I CAN SPARE THEM.
'CUZ WE DIDN'T LOSE OUR ANIMALS.
THANK YOU, MR. BREEN.
WE DIDN'T LOSE ANY OF OUR WAGONS EITHER.
WE DIDN'T LOSE OUR WAGONS, *EDDY BREEN!*
WE *CACHED* THEM. WE'LL COME BACK FOR THEM ONE DAY!
WE DIDN'T LOSE A SINGLE THING!
AND MY LEG DOESN'T EVEN HURT ANYMORE!

CHAPTER 10
SEPTEMBER 10, 1846
BASE OF PILOT PEAK
SALT LAKE
PILOT PEAK
FORT BRIDGER
SALT LAKE DESERT
REED'S GAP
IT IS TIME TO FACE FACTS. WE DO NOT HAVE ENOUGH SUPPLIES TO FINISH THE JOURNEY.
WHAT?
WHAT ABOUT THE BARRELS OF BACON?
ALL EATEN. THEY'VE BEEN TRAVELING HARD FOR FOUR MONTHS.
WE NEED VOLUNTEERS TO RIDE AHEAD AND BRING SUPPLIES BACK. JAMES REED, WILL YOU FORM THE PARTY?
YES, INDEE--
HE WILL NOT!
HE'S RIDDEN AHEAD *ENOUGH!*
I WILL STAY WITH MY FAMILY.
I'LL GO.
AH, CHARLES STANTON.
I'M A BACHELOR, I'VE GOT NOBODY TO TAKE CARE OF, I'LL GO.
IF YOU HAVE NO FAMILY WITH US, WHY WOULD YOU COME BACK?
I GIVE YOU MY WORD I WILL RETURN.
I'LL GO.
AND WILLIAM McCUTCHEON.
IF YOU PROMISE TO TAKE CARE OF MY WIFE AND DAUGHTER.
GIVE THEM ROOM IN A WAGON AND I'LL GO.
GODSPEED, MEN. OUR FATE IS IN YOUR HANDS.

SEPTEMBER 14, 1846
FLOWERY SPRINGS
HEY! QUIT KICKING UP SO MUCH DUST!
SEPTEMBER 16, 1846
MOUND SPRINGS
YOU MOVE TOO SLOW!
SEPTEMBER 20, 1846
RUBY VALLEY
DO WE HAVE TO GO OVER THOSE MOUNTAINS?

SEPTEMBER 15, 1846
JASPER PASS
DON'T FOLLOW SO CLOSE!
SEPTEMBER 18, 1846
RUBY MOUNTAINS
IT'S THE SAME THING OVER AND OVER!
SEPTEMBER 22, 1846
OVERLAND PASS
NO, WE'RE HEADED AROUND THEM.

SEPTEMBER 27, 1846
HUMBOLDT RIVER
HEE-HEE! HOO-HOO! WHOO-HAW!
HEE-HOO! HAW-HAW! HEE-HEE-HOO!
I THINK DAD IS GOING CRAZY.
HE'S REALLY LOST IT.
GOOD HEAVENS, JAMES! WHAT IS WRONG WITH YOU?
THAT'S THE HU-HUM-HUM-HUMBOLDT RIVER!
WE MADE IT THROUGH! WE'RE GOING TO CALIFORNIA!
DEAR, PLEASE--
IT'S THE TRAIL!
DON'T YOU SEE?
WE'VE COME THROUGH THE HASTINGS CUTOFF!

WE MADE IT!? WE'RE IN CALIFORNIA?
NOT QUITE YET-- BUT WE'RE BACK ON THE MAIN ROAD.
WHERE'S THE WAGON TRAIN?
LONG GONE.
I WISH WE'D NEVER LEFT THE MAIN ROAD.
WE ALL DO, DEAR.
HASTINGS CUTOFF? MORE LIKE HASTINGS LONG-TRIP!
HASTINGS HELLHOLE!
THE BOOK SAID IT WOULD SAVE US 400 MILES.
THE BOOK WAS DEAD WRONG!
IT ADDED OVER 100 MILES BY MY RECKONING.
WE'RE MORE THAN A MONTH BEHIND!
DON'T BLAME ME!
CALM DOWN, JAMES! YOU ARE GOING TO HURT YOURSELF!
QUIT COMPLAINING, FOLKS. LET'S JUST GET ON THIS ROAD AND SKEDADDLE!

OCTOBER 5, 1846
SANDY RIDGE
UNHITCH YER WAGON, REED. YOU WON'T GET UP THAT HILL WITH THAT TEAM.
YOU'LL HAVE TO BORROW EVEN MORE OXEN.
MY OLD TEAM WOULDN'T HAVE TO UNHITCH AT EVERY HILL!
THEN YA SHOULDN'T HAVE LOST 'EM.
I DIDN'T LOSE THEM!
TAKES TALENT TO LOSE FORTY OXEN IN ONE NIGHT.
MY TEAMSTERS LOST MY OXEN, SNYDER!
FUNNY, FIRST YOU LOST US ON THAT FOOL'S SHORTCUT,
THEN YOU LOST YER CATTLE!
WHY YOU--
WHATCHA GONNA LOSE NEXT, REED?
MY TEMPER, IF YOU DON'T SHUT YOUR MOUTH!
REED! SNYDER! QUIT ARGUING AND UNHITCH YOUR TEAMS!
NO-GOOD, STINKING TEAMSTERS! LAZY LOUTS AND ROUSTABOUTS! AND THAT SNYDER'S THE WORST OF 'EM.
JUMPED-UP, KNOW-IT-ALL REED! BOSSING EVERY-ONE AROUND. IF THERE'S A DEAD END, HE'LL TAKE IT!

HAH! SOME TEAMSTER YOU ARE.
I'M FINISHED DOUBLE-TEAMING MY WAGON! YOU'VE BARELY STARTED!
WE'LL SEE WHO GETS TO THE TOP FIRST, REED!
COMING THROUGH!
HUH?
EAT MY DUST!
KEEP YOUR PLACE, SIR!
THIS IS MY PLACE!
YOU ARE IN MY WAY!
CRACK
JAMES, JUST LET HIM PASS!
WHISSSSHH
YEAH! LET HIM PASS, JAMES!
CRACK
QUIT WHIPPING THOSE BEASTS!
SLOW DOWN, JAMES!
ENOUGH! I'M STOPPING!
WE'LL SETTLE THIS AT THE HILLTOP, JOHN SNYDER!

YOU'VE TANGLED THE TEAMS, YOU FOOL!
JAMES, BE CAREFUL!
DON'T YOU CUT MY LINES, JAMES REED!
YOU TANGLED THEM!
I'LL WHIP YOU GOOD.
FWISSSSH
CRACK
MARGARET!
STRIKE MY WIFE, WILL YOU!?
DROP THAT WHIP!
I'LL DROP YOU!!
WHACK

YOU DEVIL! YOU'VE WHIPPED YOUR LAST!
YOU ASKED FOR THIS, REED!
PUNCH
WHUMP
CRACK
CRUMP
ERK.
THUNK
I AM DEAD.

VIRGINIA?
WHERE ARE YOU?
I CAN'T SEE.
HERE IS A CLOTH.
HOLY COW! HE KILLED THAT GUY!?
HE DID. JAMES REED KILLED JOHN SNYDER.
I DID NOT SEE THAT COMING.
I DID. JAMES REED IS A TICKING TIME BOMB.
WELL, SNYDER WAS HITTING EVERY-ONE WITH THAT WHIP.
HE'S AN OXEN TEAM DRIVER--THAT'S HIS JOB!
IT'S HIS JOB TO WHIP MRS. REED?
NO! BUT THIS IS REED'S FAULT!
SNYDER STARTED IT!
NONSENSE!
WE'LL SETTLE THIS NOW!
HEY! HEY! STOP THAT!
SEE WHERE FIGHTING GETS YOU?
SORRY.
ALTHOUGH REED DEALT THE KILLING STROKE,
THEY WERE BOTH AT FAULT. THEY LET THEIR TEMPERS GET THE BEST OF THEM.
NOW ANOTHER MEMBER OF THE DONNER PARTY LIES DEAD.

APOLOGIZE FOR MY
CTIONS. I HAVE GIVEN
OOD FROM MY WAGON
FOR JOHN'S COFFIN.
YOU THINK THAT'S PENANCE ENOUGH? YOU KILLED SNYDER! OUR TEAMSTER! OUR FRIEND!
VE HAFF ONLY ONE CHOICE. VE MUST HANG HIM!
OH BOY!
A HANGING STORY INSIDE A HANGING STORY!
HE WAS DEFENDING ME! YOU CAN'T HANG HIM!
HE IS A MURDERER!
WHO WILL DRIVE MY TEAM NOW?
WE CAN'T JUSTIFY KILLING ANOTHER MEMBER OF OUR OWN PARTY!
MAY I SPEAK?
YOU HAFF SPOKEN ENOUGH!
HANG HIM!
WE CAN'T HANG MR. REED.
BUT WE CAN'T LET HIM STAY WITH US, EITHER.
WHAT ARE YOU GOING TO DO WITH HIM?
HE IS BANISHED.
I WILL ACCEPT THAT.
YOU CAN'T--
YOU WILL RIDE AHEAD.
YOU WILL BRING BACK SUPPLIES.
IF YOU RETURN WITH SUPPLIES, THEY'LL FORGIVE YOU!
BUT YOU BETTER GO NOW--
BEFORE THEY HANG YOU!
YOU ARE A WISE WOMAN.

YOU ARE BANISHED FROM THE PARTY--
NO HORSE! NO GUNS!
YOU MAY TAKE YOUR HORSE.
CHILDREN, SAY GOOD-BYE TO YOUR FATHER.
BYE, POPPA.
GOOD-BYE.
DO NOT FEAR, CHILDREN. I SHALL RETURN.
WE'LL ALL GET TO CALIFORNIA TOGETHER.
I DON'T WANNA GO TO CALIFORNIA!
POPPA, IT'S ME, VIRGINIA.
I'VE BROUGHT YOUR GUNS. I DON'T CARE WHAT THEY SAY.
BLESS YOU, VIRGINIA.
I'LL COME WITH YOU!
NO, DEAR, YOU MUST STAY AND HELP YOUR MOTHER.
THANK YOU FOR THE GUNS. YOU MAY HAVE SAVED MY LIFE.
DON'T CRY. WE'LL BE TOGETHER AGAIN SOON.
GOOD-BYE, POPPA.
THIS TRIP ISN'T GOING VERY WELL.
JUST WATCH. IT GETS WORSE.

CHAPTER
11
OCTOBER 11, 1846
HUMBOLDT RIVER
RUBY MOUNTAINS
HUMBOLDT RIVER
FORT BRIDGER
WHY DO WE HAVE TO LEAVE OUR WAGON?
BECAUSE THE BREENS NEED THEIR OXEN BACK.
MOMMA, DO YOU THINK POPPA'S FOUND ANY FOOD YET?
I HOPE SO.
MAYBE HE'LL MEET MR. McCUTCHEON AND MR. STANTON COMING BACK WITH FOOD.
MAYBE.
THIEVES!
PAIUTES IN THE NIGHT!
THEY STOLE MOST OF MR. DONNER'S CATTLE!
MINE TOO!
ALL OF MY HORSES ARE GONE!
THEY SNUCK RIGHT INTO CAMP AND OX-NAPPED EIGHTEEN CATTLE!
AND *ALL* OF MR. GRAVES'S HORSES!
WE HAVE TO GET OUT OF HERE! THIS PLACE IS DANGEROUS!
EVERYWHERE IS DANGEROUS.
WE NEED TO POST MORE GUARDS. WE CAN'T LOSE *ANY MORE* ANIMALS!

THE NEXT MORNING
GOOD GRIEF.
THAT'S ALL OF MR. EDDY'S TEAM AND MOST OF MR. WOLFINGER'S.
EVERYONE, BREAK CAMP. WE LEAVE NOW!
QUICKLY. THOSE ARROWS MIGHT BE TRAINED ON US NEXT.
MY TEAM IS DEAD. HOW WILL I PULL MY WAGON?
LEAVE IT, WILLIAM EDDY. WE DON'T HAVE ANIMALS TO SPARE.
COME ALONG, DEARS. IT LOOKS LIKE WE'RE ON FOOT NOW.
I MUST BURY MY VAGON!
GO ON AHEAD.
VE VILL HELP MR. VOLFINGER BURY HIS VAGON.
LOOK! IT'S A NOTE FROM POPPA!
HOORAY! WHAT DOES IT SAY?
"FORTY-MILE DESERT AHEAD, HOSTILE INDIANS."
WELL, THAT'S HAPPY NEWS.

OCTOBER 14, 1846 BOILING SPRING
FORTY MILES THROUGH THE DESERT, WE FINALLY FIND A SPRING, AND IT'S BOILING HOT!
AND IT STINKS TOO!
THIS PLACE IS SCARY.
KNOW WHAT I MISS?
HOUSES.
LET IT COOL, AND DRINK ALL YOU CAN.
YUCK! THIS WATER IS HORRIBLE!
DRINK IT ANYWAY.
THE GERMANS HAVE RETURNED.
WHERE IS MR. WOLFINGER?
ZE INDIANS. ZEY KILL HIM.
YAH. IT VAS ZE INDIANS.
VE DIDN'T KILL HIM.
THOSE TWO LOOK AWFULLY SHIFTY.
FOR GOOD REASON. INDIANS DIDN'T KILL WOLFINGER, THOSE TWO DID.
WHY?
MR. WOLFINGER WAS KNOWN TO CARRY A GREAT DEAL OF GOLD IN HIS COAT.
AUGUSTUS SPITZER AND JOSEPH REINHARDT MURDERED WOLFINGER FOR HIS GOLD.
YEESH. MURDER NUMBER TWO!
ACTUALLY, IT'S NUMBER THREE, SORT OF...
DO TELL!

FIVE DAYS EARLIER, AN OLD MAN NAMED HARDCOOP--
HARDCOOP?
HARDCOOP? IS THAT HIS FIRST OR LAST NAME?
NOBODY KNOWS. HE WAS A LONE BELGIAN MAN, PICKED UP AT FORT BRIDGER.
HE SPOKE NO ENGLISH AND RODE WITH THE GERMAN WAGONS.
FIVE DAYS AGO, MR. KESEBERG KICKED HARDCOOP OUT OF HIS WAGON.
AUSSTEIGEN UND ZU FUß!
HE FALLS BEHIND AND IS LEFT IN THE DESERT.
ICH BIN VERLOREN!
WHERE'S HARDCOOP?
BACK ON ZE ROAD! HE VILL DARKEN MY VAGON NO LONGER!
YOU LEFT HIM TO DIE!? YOU MONSTER!
I'LL GO GET HIM. I JUST NEED A HORSE.
SOMEBODY LOAN ME A HORSE--PLEASE!
ANYONE?
NOBODY LOANS WILLIAM EDDY A HORSE.
FINE! I'LL WALK BACK!
SO WILL I!
ME TOO!
GO AHEAD. BUT WE CAN'T WAIT FOR YOU.
IN THE END, NOBODY RETURNS FOR HARDCOOP. HE IS LEFT FOR DEAD.
THE MEMBERS OF THE DONNER PARTY ARE SO CLOSE TO THEIR DESTINATION.
MONTHS ON ROAD:
5
MILES TRAVELED:
2,000
MILES TO GO:
70
BUT SUPPLIES ARE SHORT,
AND SO ARE TEMPERS.
THERE'S REED'S GAP!
THEY HAVE CROSSED THE GREAT PLAINS,
THE ROCKY MOUNTAINS,
THE GREAT SALT LAKE DESERT,
AND THE RUBY MOUNTAINS.
BUT THERE IS ONE FINAL RANGE BETWEEN THEM AND SAFETY,
THE SIERRA NEVADA.

OCTOBER 20, 1846
TRUCKEE MEADOWS
WILLIAM FOSTER, WE SHOULD SEND MORE RIDERS AHEAD FOR SUPPLIES.
ME AND WILL PIKE CAN RIDE AHEAD TO FORT SUTTER.
STANTON AND McCUTCHEON RODE AHEAD, AND SO DID REED-- BUT NONE HAVE RETURNED!
WE CAN GO AHEAD AND MEET THEM.
I'M SURE THEY'RE CLOSE.
ARE THEY CLOSE?
WITH THEIR LUCK?
I SUSPECT STANTON AND McCUTCHEON WERE KILLED BY INDIANS.
AND JAMES REED IS LOST.
NO, SIR! I BET STANTON AND McCUTCHEON ARE RIGHT AROUND THE NEXT BEND--
WITH LOADS OF FOOD FOR EVERYONE!
AND REED?
OH, LOST. DEFINITELY LOST.
AIN'T NO INDIANS GONNA BOTHER ME. I'VE GOT MY PEPPERBOX.
LET ME SEE THAT.
BE CAREFUL, IT'S LOADED.
BANG
OH DEAR.
REST IN PEACE, WILLIAM PIKE. ASHES TO ASHES, DUST TO DUST.
MERCIFUL HEAVENS! THESE PEOPLE ARE CURSED!

OCTOBER 25, 1846
SIERRA NEVADA
INDIANS! I SEE INDIANS COMING!
THE ONES WHO STOLE MY CATTLE?
WAIT! IT'S STANTON!
CHARLES STANTON, YOU ARE A WELCOME SIGHT!
I TOLD YOU HE WAS CLOSE!
WHERE IS McCUTCHEON?
HE'S AT FORT SUTTER. HE WAS TOO SICK TO MAKE THE TRIP.
AND REED? DID YOU SEE JAMES REED?
HE'S THERE TOO. TRYING TO PUT TOGETHER A RETURN PARTY.
BLESS YOU, CHARLES STANTON!
YOU CAME BACK!
MEET SALVADOR AND LUIS, TWO VAQUEROS FROM FORT SUTTER.
THEY ARE FROM THE MIWOK TRIBE.
THEY WILL BE OUR GUIDES OVER THE MOUNTAIN.
WHERE'S THE REST OF THE PARTY?
EVERYONE'S SPREAD OUT.
THE REEDS AND DONNERS ARE BEHIND US.
EDWARD, RIDE BACK AND SPREAD THE NEWS.
STANTON IS BACK!
AND I'VE BROUGHT FOOD!
HOORAY FOR STANTON!
WHAT AN HONORABLE FELLOW!
HE KEPT HIS WORD. EVEN THOUGH HE HAD NO FAMILY IN THE DONNER PARTY, HE CAME BACK.

SSSSSSSS
WHOK
WHAT?
OH NO! NOT AGAIN!
SSSSSS
WHOK
WHAT'S GOING ON?
INDIANS ARE SHOOTING THE CATTLE!
WHOCK
WE CAN'T LOSE ANY MORE!
THESE OXEN ARE ALL WE HAVE! STOP!
STOP IT!
WHOK
GET DOWN EDDY!
I SEE HIM.
CRACK
GOT HIM.
ONE LONE FELLOW, NINETEEN OXEN HIT!
HE WAS A GOOD SHOT.
I'M A GOOD SHOT TOO.

THIS STORY IS DANGEROUS!
IT'S KILLED OFF FOUR PEOPLE IN FIVE PAGES!
WOLFINGER, HARDCOOP, PIKE, AND THE LONE ARCHER.
I HOPE NOBODY DIES ON THIS PAGE.
IS SUTTER'S FORT NICE, MR. STANTON?
IT IS A HAPPY SIGHT.
YOUR FATHER WAS VERY GLAD TO SEE IT.
TELL US MORE ABOUT POPPA.
WELL, YOUR POPPA CAME IN ON FOOT, TIRED AND HUNGRY.
HE HAD BEEN LIVING OFF OF BEANS SPILLED BY THE HASTINGS WAGONS.
POPPA FOLLOWED A TRAIL OF BEANS?
I GUESS YOU COULD SAY THAT.
IT MIGHT BE THE ONLY GOOD TRAIL HASTINGS EVER LEFT!
AT GEORGE DONNER'S WAGON
BOY, THIS IS STEEP!
STANTON SAYS THAT THIS SIDE IS SHARP AND ROCKY, BUT THE OTHER SIDE IS GENTLE--
CRASH
OH NO!
IS EVERYONE SAFE?
WHERE ARE GEORGIA AND LITTLE ELIZA?
HERE THEY ARE, SAFE AND SOUND.
PHEW! WE MADE IT THROUGH A PAGE WITHOUT ANYONE GETTING KILLED!

OH STRIFE! THE AXLE'S BUSTED!
MR. STANTON SAYS WE'RE CLOSE, GEORGE.
MAYBE WE SHOULD JUST LEAVE THE WAGON.
NOT A CHANCE!
I DIDN'T HAUL THIS BLASTED WAGON HALFWAY ACROSS CREATION JUST TO ABANDON IT FIFTY MILES SHORT OF SUTTER'S FORT!
WE'LL HAVE TO MAKE A NEW AXLE.
ELITHA, FETCH DADDY'S AX!
OCTOBER 31, 1846 SIERRA NEVADA
IT'S LIKE WE'RE IN A CLOUD!
WE ARE IN A CLOUD.
I WANT TO SLEEP ON A CLOUD!
IF WE'RE LUCKY, WE'LL SLEEP IN A CABIN TONIGHT.
REALLY?
THERE'S A LITTLE CABIN UP AHEAD AT TRUCKEE LAKE.
AWW! THE BREENS ARE WAY AHEAD OF US-- I BET THEY'LL STEAL THE CABIN.
I'D RATHER HAVE A CLOUD THAN A CABIN.
FAITH AND BEGORRA! IT'S A WEE CABIN!
WE'LL SLEEP HERE TONIGHT!

NOVEMBER 2, 1846
TRUCKEE LAKE
CURSE THIS RAIN!
THIS CABIN'S AWFULLY CROWDED.
AT LEAST WE'RE INSIDE!
WHERE ARE THE DONNERS!?
GEORGE IS FIXING HIS AXLE. HE'LL CATCH UP.
I DON'T WANT TO BRAVE THE PASS IN THIS RAIN.
RAIN IS BETTER THAN SNOW!
THERE'S ALREADY PLENTY OF SNOW IN THAT PASS!
SIT TIGHT, THE RAIN WILL MELT THE SNOW!
WE SHOULD GO. WE SHOULD GO NOW.
ONE MORE DAY. WE'LL WAIT OUT THE RAIN AND LET THE DONNERS CATCH UP.
NOVEMBER 3, 1846
TRUCKEE LAKE
IT DIDN'T MELT THE SNOW.
THAT'S IT! WE LEAVE NOW!
HITCH UP THE WAGONS!
WAGONS?
DON'T BE SILLY! NO WAGON WILL MAKE IT THROUGH THAT SNOW!
PACK WHAT YOU CAN ON YOUR OXEN.

IT'S TOO DEEP!
IT'S ONLY GOING TO GET DEEPER!
WAIT RIGHT HERE. WE'LL GO SCOUT THE FINAL ASCENT!
SALVADOR, COME WITH ME. WE'LL BLAZE A PATH!
ALMOST THERE!
WE MADE IT!
IT'S ALL DOWNHILL FROM HERE!
BOY, WE CUT THIS CLOSE!
A FEW MORE FEET OF SNOW AND WE'D BE TRAPPED UP HERE.
THAT WOULD BE BAD.
WHERE IS EVERYONE? WE NEED TO CROSS OVER NOW!
DID THEY GO BACK DOWN?
WHY WOULD THEY DO THAT?

THERE THEY ARE. THEY'VE GOT A FIRE GOING.
THINK IT'S BIG ENOUGH?
THE PASS CAN BE REACHED! BUT WE MUST GO NOW.
IT'S LATE.
THE CHILDREN CAN GO NO FARTHER.
WE'LL CROSS THE PASS IN THE MORNING.
YOU DON'T UNDERSTAND. IF ANY MORE SNOW FALLS, WE'LL BE TRAPPED UP HERE FOR GOOD!
UP! EVERYONE UP!
WE'LL MARCH TONIGHT AND CAMP ON THE OTHER SIDE!
DO YOU SEE THE RING AROUND THE MOON?
THAT MEANS BIG SNOW.
SOUNDS LIKE INDIAN NONSENSE TO ME.
GET UP NOW!
WE'VE UNPACKED THE ANIMALS!
STANTON, THESE CHILDREN CAN'T TAKE ANOTHER STEP!
WE'LL MARCH IN THE MORNING.
WITH ANY LUCK, THE SNOW WON'T FALL TONIGHT.

CHAPTER
12
NOVEMBER 3, 1846
SIERRA NEVADA

I CAN'T BREATHE!
POOF
SALVADOR, IS THERE ANY CHANCE WE CAN STILL GET THROUGH THE PASS?
NO, SIR. NO CHANCE.
WE SHOULD GO BACK DOWN TO THE LAKE.
BACK TO OUR CABIN!
WE CAN WAIT THERE UNTIL THIS SNOW MELTS.
THAT SNOW WON'T MELT UNTIL SPRING!
IT'S EARLY NOVEMBER. THERE IS STILL A CHANCE FOR WARM, SUNNY DAYS.
WHY, OH WHY DIDN'T THEY LISTEN TO STANTON?
THAT'S THE THOUGHT ON EVERYONE'S MIND AS THEY SET UP SHELTERS TO WAIT OUT THE SNOW.
IT SNOWS FOR EIGHT DAYS.
THEY REALLY SHOULD HAVE CROSSED THE PASS.

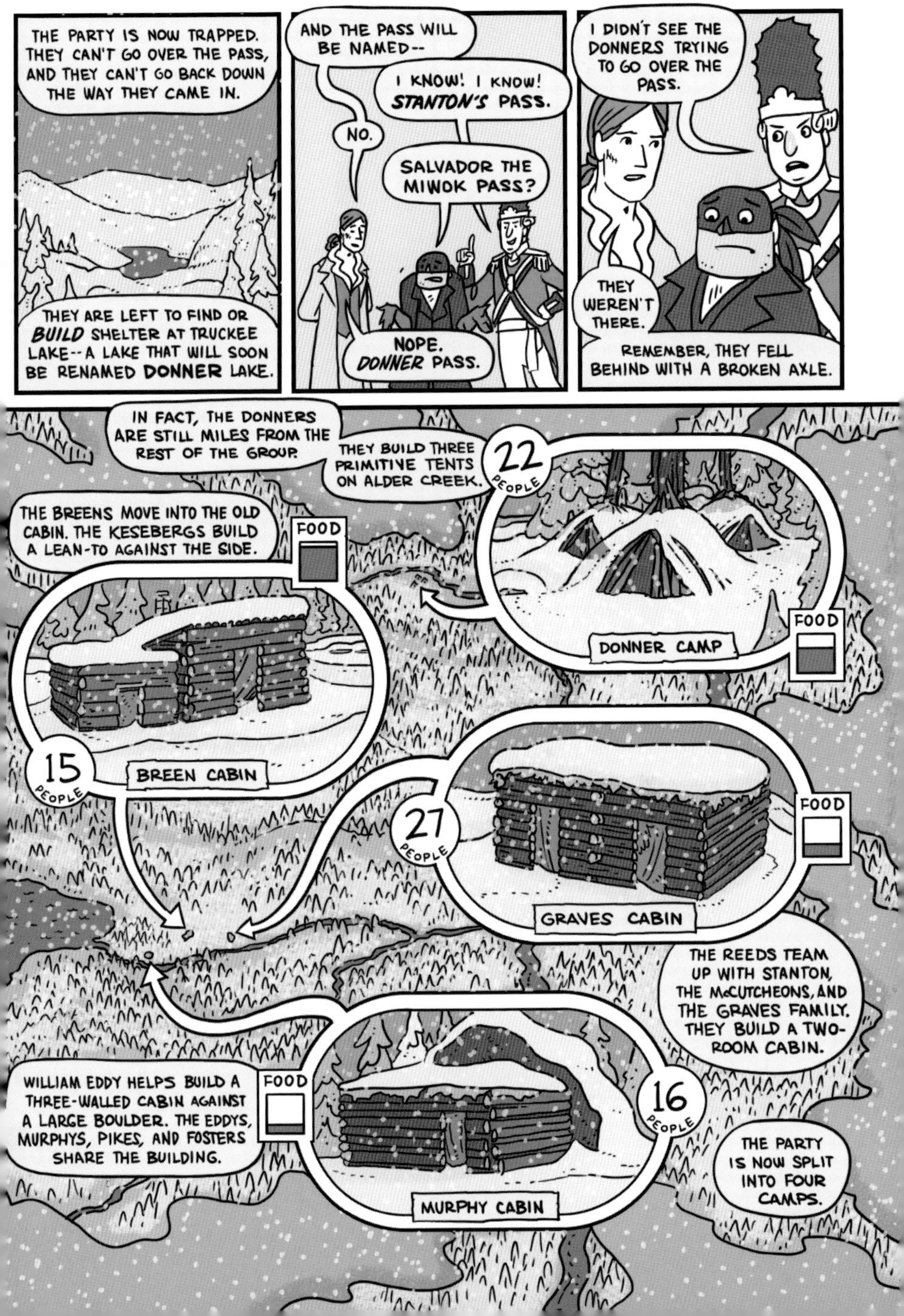

THE PARTY IS NOW TRAPPED. THEY CAN'T GO OVER THE PASS, AND THEY CAN'T GO BACK DOWN THE WAY THEY CAME IN.
THEY ARE LEFT TO FIND OR BUILD SHELTER AT TRUCKEE LAKE--A LAKE THAT WILL SOON BE RENAMED DONNER LAKE.
AND THE PASS WILL BE NAMED--
I KNOW! I KNOW! STANTON'S PASS.
NO.
SALVADOR THE MIWOK PASS?
NOPE. DONNER PASS.
I DIDN'T SEE THE DONNERS TRYING TO GO OVER THE PASS.
THEY WEREN'T THERE.
REMEMBER, THEY FELL BEHIND WITH A BROKEN AXLE.
IN FACT, THE DONNERS ARE STILL MILES FROM THE REST OF THE GROUP.
THEY BUILD THREE PRIMITIVE TENTS ON ALDER CREEK.
22 PEOPLE
DONNER CAMP
FOOD
THE BREENS MOVE INTO THE OLD CABIN. THE KESEBERGS BUILD A LEAN-TO AGAINST THE SIDE.
FOOD
15 PEOPLE
BREEN CABIN
27 PEOPLE
GRAVES CABIN
FOOD
THE REEDS TEAM UP WITH STANTON, THE McCUTCHEONS, AND THE GRAVES FAMILY. THEY BUILD A TWO-ROOM CABIN.
WILLIAM EDDY HELPS BUILD A THREE-WALLED CABIN AGAINST A LARGE BOULDER. THE EDDYS, MURPHYS, PIKES, AND FOSTERS SHARE THE BUILDING.
FOOD
16 PEOPLE
MURPHY CABIN
THE PARTY IS NOW SPLIT INTO FOUR CAMPS.

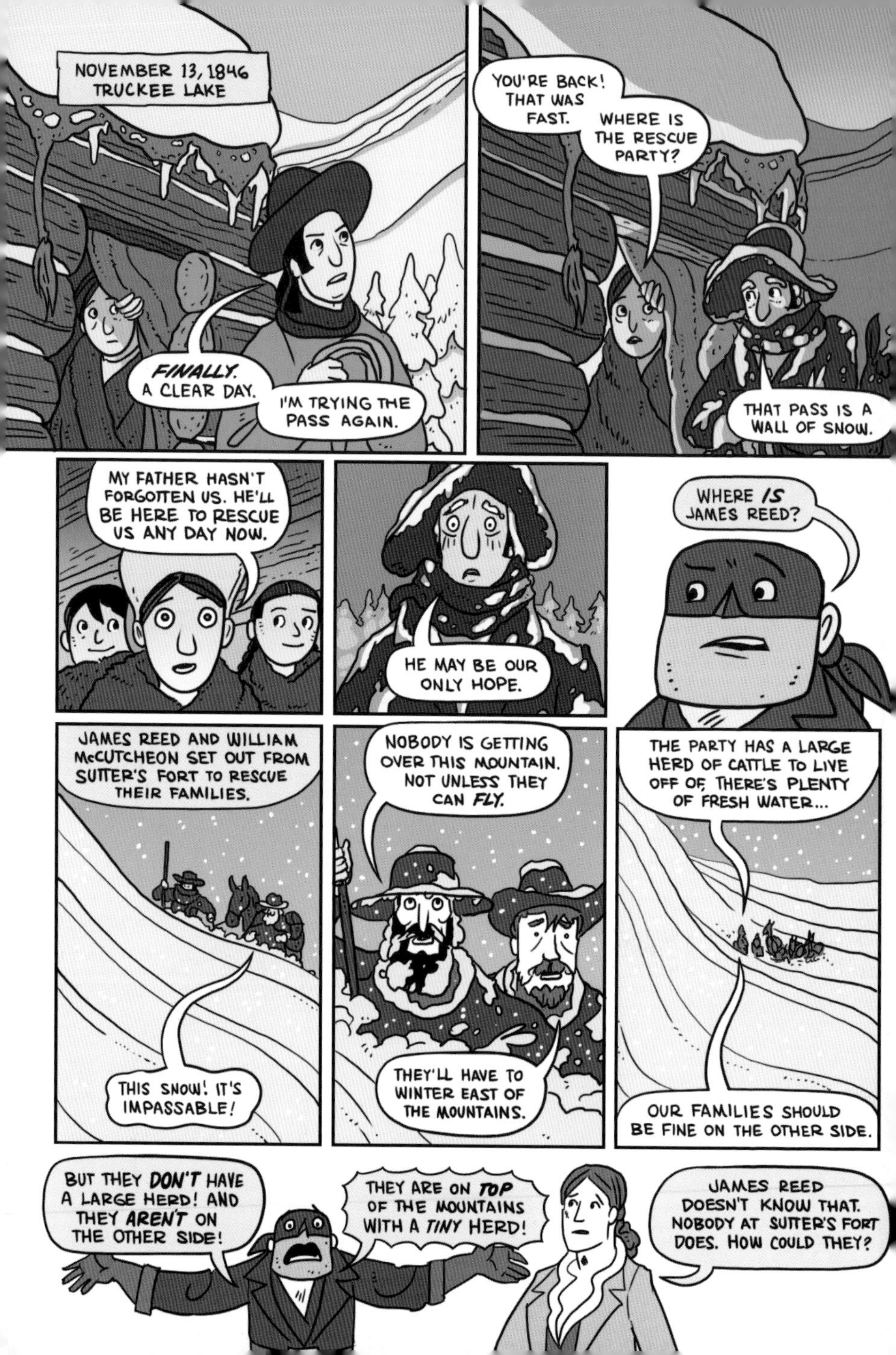
NOVEMBER 13, 1846
TRUCKEE LAKE
FINALLY. A CLEAR DAY.
I'M TRYING THE PASS AGAIN.
YOU'RE BACK! THAT WAS FAST.
WHERE IS THE RESCUE PARTY?
THAT PASS IS A WALL OF SNOW.
MY FATHER HASN'T FORGOTTEN US. HE'LL BE HERE TO RESCUE US ANY DAY NOW.
HE MAY BE OUR ONLY HOPE.
WHERE IS JAMES REED?
JAMES REED AND WILLIAM McCUTCHEON SET OUT FROM SUTTER'S FORT TO RESCUE THEIR FAMILIES.
THIS SNOW! IT'S IMPASSABLE!
NOBODY IS GETTING OVER THIS MOUNTAIN. NOT UNLESS THEY CAN FLY.
THEY'LL HAVE TO WINTER EAST OF THE MOUNTAINS.
THE PARTY HAS A LARGE HERD OF CATTLE TO LIVE OFF OF, THERE'S PLENTY OF FRESH WATER...
OUR FAMILIES SHOULD BE FINE ON THE OTHER SIDE.
BUT THEY DON'T HAVE A LARGE HERD! AND THEY AREN'T ON THE OTHER SIDE!
THEY ARE ON TOP OF THE MOUNTAINS WITH A TINY HERD!
JAMES REED DOESN'T KNOW THAT. NOBODY AT SUTTER'S FORT DOES. HOW COULD THEY?

NOVEMBER 15, 1846
TRUCKEE LAKE
FOOD STORES ARE LOW, AND GETTING LOWER.
WILLIAM EDDY HEADS OUT DAILY, HUNTING.
SO FAR, HE'S FOUND SOME SMALL GAME--A COYOTE AND AN OWL.
THAT'S NOT AN OWL!
ONE SHOT. MAKE IT COUNT.
BLAM
OH NO!
ONE MORE SHOT! ONE MORE SHOT!
RWAARRR
CLICK
BLAM
BEAR MEAT TONIGHT!
NOVEMBER 21, 1846
TRUCKEE LAKE
THE WEATHER'S BEEN CLEAR FOR DAYS. LET'S TRY THE PASS AGAIN.
MIDNIGHT, THE NEXT DAY.
WELL? ANY LUCK?
SNOW'S TOO DEEP. THE MULES SINK.
WE SHOULD EAT THE MULES AND GO OVER ON OUR OWN.

THE BEAR MEAT DOESN'T LAST.
DEALS ARE MADE. ANIMALS ARE SOLD.
TWENTY-FIVE DOLLARS FOR AN OX CARCASS?
IS THERE MUCH MEAT ON IT?
NOT REALLY. IT DIED OF STARVATION.
CATTLE ARE BUTCHERED. THE BEEF IS STORED IN THE SNOW.
EVERYTHING IS CAREFULLY RATIONED.
HUNGER GROWS.
DAYS TURN
INTO WEEKS.
SNOW FALLS.
HUNGER GROWS STRONGER.
HOPE BEGINS TO FADE.

DECEMBER 1, 1846
TRUCKEE LAKE
WILL THESE STORMS EVER STOP?
WHERE'S MY MULE TEAM?
WHERE ARE THE CATTLE?
IT WAS INDIANS!
MAYBE THEY JUST WANDERED OFF IN THE STORM!
GONE! THE LIVESTOCK IS *ALL GONE!*
WE SHOULD HAVE EATEN THEM WHEN WE HAD THE CHANCE!
DECEMBER 13, 1846
TRUCKEE LAKE
WHY ARE YOU BREAKING UP THE YOKES?
NO MORE OXEN, WE DON'T *NEED* YOKES.
THESE ARE GOING TO BE *SNOWSHOES!*
NOT QUITE AS GOOD AS THE SNOWSHOES I HAD GROWING UP IN VERMONT,
BUT THEY MAY GET US OVER THAT BLASTED PASS.
WE HAVE ENOUGH FOOD FOR A *SIX*-DAY JOURNEY.
SOMEBODY HAS TO ALERT SUTTER'S FORT.
IT'S A FORLORN HOPE, BUT WE HAVE TO TRY.

CHAPTER
13
TWELVE MEN AND FIVE WOMEN SET OUT ON THE "FORLORN HOPE EXPEDITION."
THAT'S A GLOOMY NAME. THEY SHOULD CALL IT THE "HIGH-SPEED RESCUE EXPEDITION."
THE "I CAN'T BELIEVE WE FOUND SO MUCH FOOD EXPEDITION."
WILLIAM MURPHY, 11
LEMUEL MURPHY, 12
CHARLES BURGER, 30
SARAH FOSDICK, 27
JAY FOSDICK, 23
SARAH FOSTER, 23
WILLIAM FOSTER, 28

AMANDA
CUTCHEON, 24
HARRIET
PIKE, 21
ANTONIO, 26
PATRICK
DOLAN, 35
MARY ANN
GRAVES, 19
FRANKLIN
GRAVES, 57
CHARLES
STANTON, 35
LUIS, 19
SALVADOR, 28
FOURTEEN OF THE SEVENTEEN WEAR SNOWSHOES MADE BY FRANKLIN GRAVES. CHARLES BURGER AND THE TWO YOUNGEST, LEMUEL AND WILLIAM MURPHY, PLAN TO FOLLOW *WITHOUT* SNOWSHOES.
CHARLES BURGER AND WILLIAM MURPHY TURN BACK ON THE FIRST DAY.
LEMUEL STAYS WITH THE GROUP.

I WISH I COULD GO.
I'M TIRED OF BEING STUCK HERE ALL DAY.
YOU WOULD FREEZE ON THE MOUNTAIN.
I'M FREEZING *HERE*.
COME INSIDE, IT'S TIME FOR LUNCH.
WHAT ARE WE HAVING?
THE SAME THING WE HAVE EVERY DAY, **BOILED OX HIDE**.
I *HATE* THAT GLUEY GLOP!
BE THANKFUL WE HAVE IT.
OTHER THAN THIS, ALL WE HAVE TO EAT IS **SNOW**.
I WISH WE HAD MORE BEAR MEAT.
ALL THE BEARS ARE HIBERNATING FOR THE WINTER.
I WISH *WE* COULD HIBERNATE FOR THE WINTER.
SAY, WHERE IS LITTLE **CASHY**?
I HAVEN'T SEEN HIM IN A WHILE.
CASHY IS...ER... WITH BILLY NOW.
IN A PEACEFUL MEADOW SOMEWHERE?
OR IN SOMEONE'S BELLY.

NOOOOOOO!!

THIS IS THE WORST STORY OF ALL TIME!
THIS CAN'T POSSIBLY GET ANY WORSE!
BRACE YOURSELF. IT GETS MUCH, MUCH WORSE.
IN FACT, READERS, THE NEXT PART OF THIS TALE IS NOT FOR THE FAINT OF HEART. HORRIBLE THINGS ARE GOING TO HAPPEN.
IF YOU ARE EASILY UPSET, YOU MAY WANT TO SKIP AHEAD TO PAGE 113.
DO IT! DO IT! SKIP TO PAGE 113! FOR THE LOVE OF FUZZY PUPPIES!
I CAN'T BEAR TO SEE ANY MORE CUTE LI'L ANIMALS EATEN!
OH, THEY WON'T BE EATING ANIMALS.
THEY WON'T!? WHAT A RELIEF!
WHAT DO THEY EAT?
YOU ARE ABOUT TO FIND OUT.
OR YOU CAN SK AHEAD TO 113.

DECEMBER 18, 1846 THE FORLORN HOPE EXPEDITION, DAY 3
I CAN'T SEE. I THINK I'M SNOW-BLIND.
THERE'S NOT MUCH TO SEE.
JUST SNOW. AND MORE SNOW.
THIS IS IT. WE'RE AT THE TOP.
WE'RE AS CLOSE TO HEAVEN AS WE'RE GOING TO GET.
ONE WAY OR ANOTHER.
THEY CROSSED THE PASS?
THEY DID. THE SNOWSHOES DID THE TRICK.
HOORAY!
IT'S SEVENTY MILES TO THE NEAREST SETTLEMENT.
I REALLY CAN'T SEE ANYMORE.
ARE WE FOLLOWING A BLIND GUIDE?
LUIS, SALVADOR, DOES ANYTHING LOOK FAMILIAR?
TOO MUCH SNOW. CAN'T SEE LANDMARKS.
JUST KEEP HEADING DOWN.

MEANWHILE, THE SPECTER OF DEATH STALKS THE CAMPS AT TRUCKEE LAKE.
SPECTER OF DEATH? LIKE THE GRIM REAPER?
THAT'S A REAL THING?
THE HOODED FIGURE IS SYMBOLIC, OF COURSE, BUT IN THESE SNOWY MOUNTAINS, DEATH IS VERY REAL.
DEATH TAKES BAYLIS WILLIAMS, A TEAMSTER WHO WORKED FOR THE REEDS.
I SEE HIM!
HE DIES OF A FEVER.
THINGS ARE EVEN WORSE AT ALDER CREEK.
THE DONNER TENTS ARE VERY POOR COMPARED TO THE CABINS AT THE LAKE.
THEY ARE DAMP AND NOTHING DRIES OUT, EVEN WITH FIRE.
GEORGE DONNER CUT HIS HAND WHILE FIXING HIS BROKEN AXLE. HIS ARM IS NOW DEEPLY INFECTED.
DEATH TAKES: SAM SHOEMAKER, A DONNER TEAMSTER,
JAMES SMITH, A REED TEAMSTER,
JACOB DONNER, GEORGE'S BROTHER...
AND JOSEPH REINHARDT,
WHO, DEEP IN FEVER, CONFESSES TO MURDERING JACOB WOLFINGER IN THE SALT LAKE DESERT.
WIR TÖTETEN HERR WOLFINGER!

DECEMBER 20, 1846
THE FORLORN HOPE EXPEDITION, DAY 5
COME ON, CHARLES. YOU'VE MADE THIS TRIP BEFORE--YOU CAN MAKE IT AGAIN.
LAST TIME, THERE WAS NO SNOW--AND I COULD SEE. KEEP MOVING. I'LL CATCH UP.
DECEMBER 21, 1846
THE FORLORN HOPE EXPEDITION, DAY 6
GO ON. I'LL CATCH UP.
I'M GOING TO STAY A WHILE.
HOW WILL HE CATCH UP IF HE CAN'T SEE?
HE WON'T CATCH UP.
OH.
CHARLES STANTON MADE IT ALL THE WAY TO SAFETY AT SUTTER'S FORT, THEN RETURNED TO HELP. HE KEPT HIS PROMISE.
HE DIES BY THE CAMPFIRE, PEACEFULLY SMOKING HIS PIPE, BLIND FROM THE SNOW.
THE POOR, BRAVE MAN.
THE EXPEDITION CLIMBS ON.

DECEMBER 25, 1846
TRUCKEE LAKE
I HOPE SANTA CAN FIND US HERE.
ALL I WANT IS FOOD.
CHILDREN, GATHER CLOSE. I HAVE A CHRISTMAS SURPRISE FOR ALL OF YOU.
WHAT IS IT?
I SAVED IT FOR TODAY.
BEANS, RICE, TRIPE, AND A PIECE OF BACON.
AND FOR DESSERT, A DRIED APPLE FOR EACH OF YOU.
GASP!
THIS IS THE BEST CHRISTMAS EVER!
EAT SLOWLY, BUT EAT ALL YOU WANT.
THIS IS THE BEST FOOD I EVER ET!
MMMMMMMMMMM!
EAT SLOWLY.
POPPA'S GONNA BE SAD HE MISSED THIS!

WHERE IS JAMES REED? SHOULDN'T HE BE TRYING ANOTHER RESCUE?
JAMES REED IS FIGHTING IN THE MEXICAN-AMERICAN WAR.
WHAT!?
REMEMBER, REED THINKS THE PARTY IS SAFE, SOUND, AND WELL-PROVISIONED...
ON THE OTHER SIDE OF THE MOUNTAINS.
NEARLY ALL OF THE ABLE-BODIED MEN AT SUTTER'S FORT HAVE BEEN DRAWN INTO THE WAR.
IN REED'S MIND, THE SOONER THE WAR IS WON, THE SOONER HE'LL BE ABLE TO GATHER A SUPPLY PARTY.
JANUARY 2, 1847 THE BATTLE OF SANTA CLARA A.K.A. "THE BATTLE OF THE MUSTARD STALKS"
FOLLOW ME, LADS!
THIS LOOKS LIKE A SHORTCUT TO THE BATTLEFIELD!
JAMES REED. NEVER A DULL MOMENT.

DECEMBER 25, 1846
THE FORLORN HOPE EXPEDITION, DAY 10
CHRISTMAS IN THE FORLORN HOPE EXPEDITION WASN'T AS NICE.
WHEN DEATH COMES FOR ME --AND IT WILL SOON--PROMISE ME THIS: DON'T WASTE MY FLESH.
DON'T TALK LIKE THAT, FATHER! WE'LL FEEL BETTER WHEN MR. EDDY GETS THIS FIRE LIT.
I CAN'T! I CAN'T GET A FIRE STARTED!
EVERYONE HUDDLE IN CLOSER.
I'M WARM!
SIT DOWN, PATRICK --IT'S NOT WARM!
NO, IT IS. IT'S AS WARM AS A SUMMER DAY.
PATRICK, STOP! YOU'LL FREEZE!
WHAT'S WRONG WITH HIM?
HE HAS HYPOTHERMIA. WHEN PEOPLE FREEZE TO DEATH, A FALSE SENSE OF WARMTH CAN SOMETIMES COME OVER THEM.
REALLY?
SCOOT BACK, I'M GOING TO TRY AND START A FIRE WITH POWDER.
BAM
AGH!
WHEN AT LAST A FIRE IS LIT, DEATH HAS TAKEN THREE.
DEATH TAKES PATRICK DOLAN, ANTONIO THE SHEPHERD, AND FRANKLIN GRAVES, THE SNOWSHOE MAKER.

CHAPTER 14
DECEMBER 26, 1846 THE FO[...] HOPE EXP[...]Y 11
I REALLY HATE THAT SPECTER OF DEATH.
"WOE, DESTRUCTION, RUIN AND DECAY; THE WORST IS DEATH, AND DEATH WILL HAVE HIS DAY."
THAT'S SHAKESPEARE, THAT IS.
THAT'S SCARY, THAT IS.
WHY ARE YOU SO SCARED, HANGMAN? YOU AND THE REAPER BOTH WEAR BLACK HOODS--AND YOU BOTH END LIVES.
YOU COULD BE BROTHERS.
THAT'S NO BROTHER OF MINE!
HE COULD BE YOUR TWIN! YOUR SKINNIER TWIN!
THAT'S IT!
I'M TURNING TO PAGE 113! I'VE HAD ENOUGH!
LEAVE THOSE PAGES ALONE!
I CAN'T TAKE IT! NO MORE DEATH! NO MORE DEAD PETS!
MR. KESEBERG IS NOW THE ONLY LIVING SOUL LEFT AT TRUCKEE LAKE.
WHAT!?? AAAAAA
AWWWW! YOU'VE GONE TOO FAR! THIS IS ALL OUT OF CONTEXT!

CHAPTER 14
DECEMBER 26, 1846
THE FORLORN HOPE
EXPEDITION, DAY 11
LET'S START THIS CHAPTER OVER AGAIN.
WAKE ME WHEN IT'S *OVER*.
PLUG YOUR EARS IF YOU DON'T WANT TO HEAR THE WORST.
I CAN'T HEAR YOU!
NANANANANANANANANANANANA
THE MEMBERS OF THE FORLORN HOPE EXPEDITION **COOK** AND **EAT** THE BODIES OF THE DEAD.
OH. IS THAT ALL?
YES. THEY PARTICIPATE IN CANNIBALISM.
THAT'S NOT SO BAD.
I THINK I'M GOING TO BE SICK...
I'VE DONE CANNIBALISM.
WHAT?
SURE, I WAS SHIPWRECKED ONCE. WE COOKED THE COOK.
YOU ARE A *CANNIBAL!?*
I WAS.
WE HAD TO EAT TO SURVIVE. IT'S THE CUSTOM OF THE SEA.
WHY ARE YOU LOOKING AT ME LIKE THAT? IT'S NOT LIKE I ATE A CUTE PUPPY OR ANYTHING.
I'M ABSOLUTELY SPEECHLESS.
IT SAVED MY LIFE, ALONG WITH THOSE OF THE CREW.
NOW GET TO THAT **GRIM** PART. I'LL PLUG MY EARS AGAIN.
THAT *WAS* THE GRIM PART!
CANNIBALISM! IT DOESN'T GET ANY GRIMMER!
YOU WERE MORE UPSET OVER BILLY AND CASHY THAN THE EATING OF *HUMAN FLESH!*
DON'T SAY THEIR NAMES --IT'S STILL TOO SOON FOR ME.

CHAPTER 14
THIS CHAPTER HAS STARTED *THREE TIMES* NOW.
JUST LIKE THE THREE ATTEMPTS TO CROSS THE PASS. THIS TIME WE'LL GET OVER IT.
BECAUSE YOU KEEP INTERRUPTING IT!
JANUARY 1, 1847 THE FORLORN HOPE EXPEDITION, DAY 17
THE EXPEDITION NOW NUMBERS TEN; FIVE MEN AND FIVE WOMEN.
WAIT, **TEN**? DID DEATH TAKE ANOTHER PERSON?
YES.
FOR YOUNG LEMUEL FOSTER, THE BOY WITHOUT SNOWSHOES,
THE FOOD CAME TOO LATE.
THE FOUR BODIES ARE CAREFULLY CARVED.
THE MEAT IS COOKED AND PACKED.
WITH THEIR NEW FOOD SUPPLY, THE EXPEDITION IS ABLE TO STAY A FEW STEPS AHEAD OF DEATH.
ARE WE **LOST**?
LUIS, SALVADOR, *ARE WE LOST*?
HEY! GUIDES, WHERE ARE WE GOING?
TOO MUCH SNOW. CAN'T RECOGNIZE ANYTHING.
THEN YOU ARE GOOD FOR *NOTHING*!
CALM DOWN, MR. FOSTER!
WE SHOULD KILL THEM AND **COOK** THEM!
WE AREN'T *MURDERERS*!
AFTER HEARING WILLIAM FOSTER'S *"EAT THE MIWOKS"* PLAN, LUIS AND SALVADOR LEFT THE FORLORN HOPE.

AT TRUCKEE LAKE, FOOD SUPPLIES HAVE DWINDLED TO NEARLY NOTHING.
THE DONNERS ARE EATING MICE, WHEN THEY CAN CATCH THEM.
THE CHILDREN IN THE MURPHY CABIN HAVE EATEN THE RUG.
PATTY, JAMES, AND TOMMY ARE EATING THROUGH THE RAWHIDE ROOF OF THEIR CABIN.
CHILDREN, DON'T EAT THE ROOF! WE NEED THE ROOF!
WE NEED FOOD!
YOU COULD SAY THEY ARE EATING HER OUT OF HOUSE AND HOME!
YOU COULD.
BUT IT WOULDN'T BE VERY FUNNY.
JANUARY 10, 1847 THE FORLORN HOPE EXPEDITION, DAY 26
MARY ANN!
WHAT ARE YOU DOING!? DON'T EAT YOUR SNOWSHOES!
I'M JUST SO HUNGRY.
WE SHOULD STAGE A DUEL. THEN WE CAN EAT THE LOSER.
IF WE EVER CATCH LUIS AND SALVADOR, WE CAN EAT THEM! THE COWARDLY RUNAWAYS!
CAN YOU BLAME THEM FOR RUNNING AWAY?
LOOK! TRACKS!
THOSE AREN'T ANIMAL TRACKS--THOSE ARE RUNAWAY TRACKS.
EDDY, GO HUNT THEM DOWN!
NO. I WON'T HUNT LUIS AND SALVADOR.
FINE. I'LL GET THEM MYSELF!
DON'T...
WE...SHOULDN'T... MURDER.
BAM
BAM
COME UP HERE AND HELP ME BUTCHER THESE BODIES.
LUIS AND SALVADOR, THE TWO MIWOKS WHO VOLUNTEERED TO HELP THE DONNER PARTY, WERE HUNTED, SHOT, AND EATEN.
GOOD HEAVENS. I NEED TO LIE DOWN.

SEVEN NOW REMAIN IN THE FORLORN HOPE EXPEDITION. BESIDES LUIS AND SALVADOR, DEATH HAS ALSO TAKEN JAY FOSDICK.
DEATH DIDN'T TAKE THE MIWOKS-- WILLIAM FOSTER DID!
THAT WASN'T RIGHT. THOSE MEN CAME TO HELP!
IN A GRUESOME WAY, THEY *DID* HELP.
THE STRENGTH GAINED FROM THEIR REMAINS HELPED THE SURVIVORS TRAVEL TWO MORE DAYS,
DOWN PAST THE SNOW LINE,
AND INTO A VILLAGE.
WE CAN'T STOP HERE-- THIS IS A MIWOK VILLAGE!
WE ATE THEIR *KIN*!
WE ATE OUR *OWN* KIN!
THEY DON'T NEED TO KNOW!
YOU EAT BREAD?
OH, BLESS YOU!
I CAN'T SWALLOW. WHAT IS IN THIS?
ACORN BREAD.
I CAN'T EAT THIS.
HE CAN EAT HUMAN FLESH, BUT HE CAN'T EAT ACORNS?
ACORNS ARE PRETTY GROSS.
THE FORLORN HOPE GROUP COLLAPSES AT THE MIWOK VILLAGE, JUST A FEW STEPS AHEAD OF DEATH.
THEY HAVE ALMOST ESCAPED THE SIERRA NEVADA.

CHAPTER 15
JANUARY 5, 1847
TRUCKEE LAKE
WE WON'T LAST MUCH LONGER WITHOUT RESCUE.
WHERE ARE THE SNOWSHOERS?
OR POPPA?
I DON'T KNOW.
WE HAVE TO SEND ANOTHER GROUP.
WHO?
VIRGINIA, ELIZA WILLIAMS, MILT ELLIOT, AND ME.
WHAT ABOUT US?
PATTY AND TOMMY, YOU WILL GO TO THE BREENS' CABIN.
JAMES, STAY WITH THE GRAVESES.
I HAVE TO GO. I WILL BRING BACK FOOD AND RESCUE.
DON'T GO!
DON'T LEAVE US!
DO YOU WANT ME TO STAY, OR DO YOU WANT FOOD AND RESCUE?
I WANT BOTH!
THE FOUR SET OUT, WITH NO SNOWSHOES.
THEY LAST FOUR DAYS.
NOOOOOOO!
THEY DON'T DIE.
OH.
THEY TURN AROUND AND COME BACK.
HOORAY!
FOOD AND RESCUE!
FOOD AND RESCUE!
NOT YET, CHILDREN.
BUT AT LEAST WE'RE ALL TOGETHER AGAIN.

JANUARY 17, 1847
JOHNSON'S RANCH
MOMMY?
YES, DEAR?
THERE'S A SKELETON MAN AT THE DOOR.
DON'T BE SILLY, DEAR, THERE IS NO SUCH THING AS--
WAAAAAGH!
YOU WANT FOOD, SKELETON MAN?
YESSS.
COME WITH ME.
IS THIS SUTTER'S FORT?
NO, THIS IS JOHNSON'S RANCH, A SETTLEMENT FORTY MILES FROM THE FORT.
WILLIAM EDDY WAS GUIDED HERE BY MIWOK VILLAGERS.
HOLY MOSES! WHERE'D YOU COME FROM?
UP THE MOUNTAIN... TRAPPED... FAMILIES IN THE SNOW...
YOUR FAMILY IS STUCK ON THE MOUNTAIN?
TRUCKEE LAKE... STARVING.
IF THEY LOOK ANYTHING LIKE YOU, THEY MUST BE HALF DEAD ALREADY!
SIX MORE... ON FOOT... BEHIND ME...
YOU SAY THERE ARE SIX MORE LIKE YOU OUT THERE?
YESSS.
GATHER HORSES! BRING TORCHES AND LANTERNS!
REST EASY, BROTHER, YOU ARE SAFE NOW. EAT SOMETHING.
GOOD NIGHT, MR. SKELETON.
ZZZZ
HE DID IT! WILLIAM EDDY ESCAPED!
THE RESCUERS FOLLOW EDDY'S BLOODY FOOTPRINTS TO WHERE THE FORLORN HOPE EXPEDITION HAS COLLAPSED IN THE MUD.
WORD IS SENT TO SUTTER'S FORT.
THE RESCUE HAS BEGUN.

FEBRUARY 21, 1847 TRUCKEE LAKE, OVER A MONTH LATER
THIS IS THE DONNER CAMP, BUT I DON'T SEE ANYONE.
HELLO?
WE'RE **SAVED**!
ARE YOU FROM HEAVEN?
WE'RE FROM CALIFORNIA.
WE HAD A ROUGH TIME GETTING HERE.
WE CAN'T TAKE YOU *ALL* OUT, BUT MORE HELP IS ON THE WAY!
FOOD! DID YOU BRING FOOD?
A LITTLE. WE USED MOST OF IT GETTING HERE.
YOU FOLKS SURE PICKED A HELL OF A CAMPSITE.
ONLY HALF OF THE DONNER PARTY SURVIVORS ARE STRONG ENOUGH TO LEAVE THE CAMP.
MARGARET REED AND HER CHILDREN JOIN THE RESCUE PARTY.
THOSE WHO REMAIN IN THE CAMPS WILL EAT THE NEW RATIONS AND TRY TO REGAIN STRENGTH.
ALL THEY CAN DO NOW IS WAIT FOR THE SECOND RESCUE PARTY,
AND HOPE THAT **DEATH** DOESN'T FIND THEM FIRST.
DEATH HAS BEEN VERY BUSY IN THE HIGH CAMPS.
MILT ELLIOT
JOHN MURPHY
LEWIS KESEBERG JR.
AUGUSTUS SPITZER
HARRIET McCUTCHEON
CATHERINE PIKE
MAGARET EDDY
ELEANOR EDDY
OH NO,
THAT'S WILLIAM EDDY'S WIFE AND DAUGHTER.
HOW AWFUL.

WE'RE FINALLY GOING TO CALIFORNIA!
I THOUGHT YOU DIDN'T WANT TO GO TO CALIFORNIA.
ANYWHERE IS BETTER THAN HERE.
KEEP GOING, PATTY.
I CAN'T, TOMMY. I CAN'T GO ANY FARTHER.
THESE TWO WON'T MAKE IT UP THE PASS.
THEN WE'LL GO BACK TOO.
KEEP CLIMBIN', MA'AM. THEY DON'T NEED ANY MORE MOUTHS TO FEED AT THE CAMPS.
THOSE KIDS'LL HAVE TO COME OUT WITH THE NEXT RESCUE PARTY.
WE HAVE TO GO BACK?
YOU'LL BE SAFE WITH THE BREENS.
STAY WITH THEM UNTIL THE NEXT RESCUE PARTY COMES.
GOOD-BYE, MOMMA. IF I DON'T SEE YOU AGAIN, JUST DO THE BEST YOU CAN.
SHE'S SUCH A BRAVE LITTLE GIRL.
COME ON, TOMMY. WE AREN'T GOING TO CALIFORNIA.
ARE WE GOING TO DIE?
WE MIGHT.
I HOPE NOT.
SAY THEY DON'T! OH, SAY THEY *DON'T!*
THEY DON'T.
THANK GOODNESS!
THEY **WILL** EAT THE FLESH OF THE DEAD WHEN ALL OTHER FOOD RUNS OUT AT THE CAMPS.
GOOD! THAT MEANS THEY'LL *SURVIVE*.
THEY WILL ALSO EAT THE BREENS' DOG, TOWSER.
NOOOOOOOOOO

THE RESCUE PARTY IS NO GUARANTEE OF SAFETY.
DEATH FOLLOWS CLOSELY.
KEEP MOVING EVERYONE! DON'T LET OL' BONE-FACE CATCH YOU!
JOHN DENTON, ADA KESEBERG
I CAN'T TAKE ANOTHER STEP.
YES, YOU CAN, JAMES. EACH STEP BRINGS YOU CLOSER TO POPPA... AND FOOD.
THAT'S THE WAY.
IT WORKED! THERE HE IS!
WHO?
POPPA!
MY DEAR FAMILY!
HUH.
POPPA!
WHERE IS EVERYONE?
MOMMA FAINTED--
--AND PATTY AND TOMMY ARE BACK AT THE CAMP.
JAMES, IS IT REALLY YOU?
IT'S REALLY ME!
I DIDN'T THINK I'D EVER SAY IT, BUT I'M HAPPY TO SEE THAT CRAZY BEARDED FACE.
WHEN JAMES REED HEARD THE REPORTS OF THE FORLORN HOPE EXPEDITION, HE IMMEDIATELY RALLIED A RESCUE EFFORT.
WHEN HE ARRIVES, THE KILLING OF JOHN SNYDER IS ALL BUT FORGOTTEN.
GO GET TOMMY AND PATTY!
YES, GO GET THEM!
I WON'T REST UNTIL THEY ARE SAFELY OUT!

MARCH 1, 1847
TRUCKEE LAKE
POPPA! YOU CAME!
FOOD AND RESCUE!
WAKE UP, EVERYONE! I'M HERE TO RESCUE YOU ALL!
HEY, LOOK! IT'S PAGE 113! HAPPY DAY!
AREN'T YOU GLAD YOU TURNED TO THIS PAGE AND SKIPPED THE TROUBLES?
IF YOU DID, YOU MISSED ALL OF THE CANNIBA--
HUSH! IF THEY SKIPPED TO THIS PAGE, THEY DON'T WANT TO HEAR ABOUT IT.
ONLY SEVENTEEN? I'M HERE TO RESCUE EVERYONE!
WHERE ARE THE LAST NINE?
TOO SICK TO MOVE. AND I'M STAYING TO WATCH OVER THEM.
VERY WELL, TAMSEN.
WE'LL LEAVE WHAT SUPPLIES WE CAN.
AND WE'LL FIX YOUR TENT.
THANK YOU, JAMES. SOME TRIP IT'S BEEN, EH?
THANK ME AT SUTTER'S FORT, GEORGE.
YOU'LL BE IN BETTER HEALTH WHEN THE NEXT RESCUE PARTY ARRIVES.
THREE DAYS FROM CAMP, REED'S PARTY IS TRAPPED IN A BLIZZARD.
OH, I HATE SNOW. I HATE IT SO MUCH.
WE MUST BUILD A FIRE!
THERE IS A FIRE, JAMES.
I CAN'T SEE IT.
I THINK I'VE GONE SNOW-BLIND.
OH NO! NOT THIS AGAIN!

THE BLIZZARD POUNDS REED'S GROUP FOR *DAYS*.
KEEP THE FIRE BLAZING. IT'S THE ONLY THING KEEPING US ALIVE.
THE HEAT FROM THE FLAMES CAUSES THE SNOW BENEATH THEM TO MELT.
THE FIRE KEEPS DEATH AT BAY.
BUT NOT FOR EVERYONE.
ISAAC DONNER, ELIZABETH GRAVES, AND FRANKLIN GRAVES JR.
THE EXHAUSTED SURVIVORS SINK DEEP INTO THE SNOW.
THEY CALL THE PIT **"STARVED CAMP."**
ONCE AGAIN THE DONNER PARTY CHOOSES THE GLOOMIEST POSSIBLE NAME.
THIS IS **AFTER** PAGE 113? THIS IS **SUPER** GRIM!
YOU'RE RIGHT, THE NEXT FEW PAGES AREN'T PLEASANT. SKIP TO PAGE 118 IF YOU CAN'T HANDLE IT.
DO YOU THINK ANYONE'S ***REALLY*** SKIPPING THE GROSS PARTS?
OF COURSE NOT. THIS IS A BOOK ABOUT ***THE DONNER PARTY.*** READERS WANT ALL THE GORY BITS.
WHEN THE STORM CLEARS, SO DOES JAMES REED'S BLINDNESS.
I CAN SEE! WE SHOULD GO ***NOW,*** WHILE THE STORM HAS BROKEN.
WE CAN'T GO ON. WE'LL WAIT RIGHT HERE.
WE MUST STAY!
WE MUST GO!
STAYING HERE IS A *DEATH SENTENCE!*
WE ARE IN NO SHAPE TO MARCH. YOU ESCAPED A DEATH SENTENCE ONCE, JAMES REED. WE WILL TOO.
VERY WELL, THEN. WE WILL LEAVE YOU WITH THREE DAYS' WORTH OF FIREWOOD.
PRAY THAT RESCUE ARRIVES IN THAT TIME.
WE WILL PRAY.
REED MOVES ON WITH PATTY, TOMMY, AND FIVE OTHERS.
THE BREEN FAMILY HAS SURVIVED EVERYTHING-- ONLY TO END UP HERE.

ARCH 14, 1847
TARVED CAMP
THE BREENS LIVE IN THE PIT FOR A WEEK.
THEY ARE SUSTAINED BY THE BODIES OF THE DEAD.
STARVED CAMP SINKS THROUGH FIFTEEN FEET OF SNOW, ALL THE WAY TO BARE GROUND.
AND HERE COMES DEATH.
OH, THOSE POOR BREEN KIDS!
WAIT--THAT'S NOT DEATH, IT'S WILLIAM EDDY.
HELLO, BREENS--WHAT ARE YOU DOING DOWN THERE?
PRAYING FOR A RESCUE PARTY. ARE YOU IT?
WE ARE. LET'S GET YOU OUT OF THAT HOLE.
EVERYONE FROM STARVED CAMP HEADS OUT WITH THE RESCUERS.
WILLIAM EDDY AND WILLIAM FOSTER CONTINUE ON TO TRUCKEE LAKE.
WHAT A HORRIBLE SIGHT.
THEY SEARCH THE CAMP FOR THEIR FAMILIES, BUT THEY ARE GONE.
TAKEN BY DEATH.
JAMES EDDY
GEORGE FOSTER
LEWIS DONNER
THEY DON'T STAY LONG. THEY TAKE THE LAST SURVIVORS AND LEAVE. FIVE STAY BEHIND.
WHY ON EARTH DID THEY STAY?
GEORGE DONNER IS AT DEATH'S DOOR, SO IS SAMMY DONNER. TAMSEN REFUSES TO LEAVE.
LAVINIA MURPHY IS TOO SICK TO MOVE AND LEWIS KESEBERG HAS AN INJURED FOOT.
DOESN'T EVERYONE HAVE INJURED FEET BY NOW?
FIVE STAY AT THE DESOLATE CAMP. ONLY ONE WILL SURVIVE.
IT'S OBVIOUSLY TAMSEN, RIGHT?
RIGHT?

CHAPTER
16
APRIL 19, 1847
TRUCKEE LAKE
WHEN THE FINAL RESCUE PARTY ARRIVES, WEEKS LATER, THEY FIND ONLY CORPSES,
AND LEWIS KESEBERG.
WHAT?!
I DON'T TRUST THAT GUY! I BET HE KILLED AND ATE THE OTHERS! TAMSEN WASN'T EVEN SICK!
THE RESCUERS MAKE THE SAME CONCLUSION. NEWSPAPERS WILL SAY THAT KESEBERG IS MAD, A MURDERING CANNIBAL.
LOOK AT HIM! HE MUST BE!
KESEBERG CLAIMS SHE FELL INTO A STREAM AND FROZE. BUT THERE IS NO EVIDENCE.
IT HAS BEEN EATEN.
TAMSEN'S DEATH REMAINS A MYSTERY.
RUMORS OF MURDER AND CANNIBALISM WILL FOLLOW LEWIS KESEBERG FOR THE REST OF HIS DAYS.
LADY ADAMS HOTEL
RESTAURANT
HE GOES ON TO OPEN A RESTARAUNT IN SAN FRANCISCO. IT DOESN'T DO VERY WELL.
WITH KESEBERG RESCUED, THE CAMPS ARE NOW EMPTY.
THE JOURNEY, WHICH STARTED NEARLY A YEAR AGO, IS OVER.
THE BREENS, ALL SIX BOYS, AND THE BABY GIRL HAVE ALSO REACHED CALIFORNIA SAFELY.
SUTTER'S FORT
SUTTER'S FORT
THE REED FAMILY HAS SURVIVED THE ORDEAL INTACT-- EXCEPT FOR GRANDMA KEYES.
DEATH'S FINAL TOLL FOR THE JOURNEY IS FORTY-TWO.

YOU'RE RIGHT. I'M NO LONGER HUNGRY.
FUNNY, I'M EVEN HUNGRIER NOW.
BUT ONE THING'S FOR SURE--I **NEVER** WANT TO GO TO CALIFORNIA.
IN YEARS TO COME, MANY MORE WILL MAKE THE JOURNEY.
DO THEY TAKE THE HASTINGS CUTOFF?
NO, THEY DO NOT.
A YEAR LATER, IN 1848, **GOLD** WILL BE DISCOVERED AT SUTTER'S MILL.
A YEAR AFTER THAT, TENS OF THOUSANDS OF "FORTY-NINERS" WILL TREK TO CALIFORNIA WITH GOLD RUSH FEVER.
TWENTY YEARS LATER, A RAILROAD WILL RUN FROM COAST TO COAST.
THE RAILROAD WILL MEET IN UTAH, IN THE SAME DESERT WHERE THE REEDS LOST THEIR WAGONS.
A GOLDEN SPIKE WILL MARK THE POINT WHERE THE RAILROADS MEET.
TRAINS WILL CROSS THE COUNTRY WITH EASE. GOING TO CALIFORNIA WILL TAKE DAYS, NOT MONTHS.
I DON'T UNDERSTAND ANYTHING YOU JUST SAID.
I KNOW WHAT A TRAIN IS.
YOU DO?
SURE. IT'S THAT LONG BIT OF CLOTH THAT DRAGS BEHIND THE DRESS OF A FANCY LADY.
THAT *IS* ONE DEFINITION OF THE WORD "TRAIN." I CAN'T ARGUE WITH THAT.
AND YOU SAY PEOPLE WILL RIDE 'CROSS THE COUNTRY ON THEM?
THAT I'D LIKE TO SEE!

AND THERE YOU HAVE IT. THE TRAGIC TALE OF THE DONNER PARTY.
PHEW.
IT TRULY WAS HAZARDOUS!
DIRE AND DISGUSTING, BUT A TESTAMENT TO THE HUMAN WILL TO SURVIVE.
NOT TO THE ONES WHO DIED, IT WASN'T--MORE LIKE A TESTAMENT TO **LOUSY LUCK**.
WHAT ***IS*** THE MORAL OF THIS GRISLY TALE?
I'D SAY IT'S "DON'T GO CAMPING WITH THE GRIM REAPER."
STORIES FROM HISTORY DON'T ALWAYS HAVE A ***MORAL***. BUT IF THIS ONE DOES,
VIRGINIA REED, HERSELF, PROBABLY SAID IT BEST IN A LETTER TO HER COUSIN:
"DON'T TAKE NO CUT-OFFS AND GET WHERE YOU'RE GOING AS FAST AS YOU CAN."

NH
HT

NATHAN HALE'S HAZARDOUS TALES

WHO DIED AND WHO SURVIVED

KEY: STARVATION/EXPOSURE ACCIDENTAL SHOOTIN

OLD AGE
OVEREATING
TUBERCULOSIS
MURDER
UNKNOWN
CANNIBALIZED
JAMES REED, 46
MARGARET REED, 33
VIRGINIA REED, 13
MARTHA 'PATTY' REED, 8
JAMES REED JR, 5
THOMAS REED, 4
SARAH KEYES, 70
HIRAM MILLER, 29
JAMES SMITH, 25
WALTER HERRON, 25
BAYLIS WILLIAMS, 24
ELIZA WILLIAMS, 31
WILLIAM McCUTCHEON, 30
AMANDA McCUTCHEON, 24
HARRIET McCUTCHEON, 2
AVINIA MURPHY, 50
LANDRUM MURPHY, 15
MARY MURPHY, 14
LEMUEL MURPHY, 12
WILLIAM MURPHY, 11
IMON MURPHY, 9
WILLIAM FOSTER, 28
SARAH MURPHY FOSTER, 23
GEORGE FOSTER, 4
WILLIAM PIKE, 25
ARRIET MURPHY PIKE, 21
NAOMI + CATHERINE PIKE, 2
PATRICK BREEN, 51
MARGARET BREEN, 40
JOHN BREEN, 14
EDWARD BREEN, 13
PATRICK BREEN JR, 9
SIMON BREEN, 8
JAMES BREEN, 5
PETER BREEN, 3
SABELLA BREEN, 1
CHARLES BURGER, 30
PATRICK DOLAN, 35
CHARLES STANTON, 35
ANTONIO, 26
ACOB WOLFINGER, 26
DORIS WOLFINGER, 18
HARDCOOP, 60
SALVADOR, 28
LUIS, 19

THE SAD, SAD STORY OF WILLIAM HOOK
THE BOY WHO ATE TOO MUCH

JAMES AND MARGARET REED

THE REED FAMILY SETTLED IN SAN JOSE, WHERE JAMES BECAME A RANCHER. HE ALSO SAT ON THE FIRST TOWN COUNCIL AND WAS CHIEF OF POLICE.

VIRGINIA WROTE A MEMOIR OF HER JOURNEY CALLED "*ACROSS THE PLAINS IN THE DONNER PARTY 1846*." HER DESCRIPTIONS WERE USED EXTENSIVELY WHEN RESEARCHING THIS BOOK. BILL THE PONY, SCARING SIOUX BRAVES WITH A TELESCOPE, TAKING HER FATHER'S GUNS --THESE ARE STORIES FROM VIRGINIA'S TALE.

PATTY'S TINY DOLL, NAMED "DOLLY," ALSO SURVIVED THE TRIP. DOLLY CAN BE SEEN AT SUTTER'S FORT STATE HISTORIC PARK, CA.

MARTHA "PATTY" REED

THERE WERE TWO DONNER FAMILIES--THE **GEORGE** DONNER FAMILY AND THE **JACOB** DONNER FAMILY. THE ONLY DONNERS TO MAKE IT SAFELY OVER THE PASS WERE ORPHANS: ALL FOUR DONNER PARENTS DIED AT TRUCKEE LAKE. THE DONNER ORPHANS FOUND FAMILIES IN CALIFORNIA TO LIVE WITH. MARY AND FRANCES DONNER LIVED WITH THE REEDS IN SAN JOSE. THE DONNER NAME IS NOW A PERMANENT PART OF THE LANDSCAPE OF THE AMERICAN WEST; DONNER LAKE AND DONNER PASS ARE JUST TWO OF MANY LOCATIONS NAMED FOR THE FAMILY.

ALL OF THE BREENS SURVIVED. **ALL** SEVEN CHILDREN, RANGING FROM AGES 1 TO 14, MADE IT THROUGH THE DEADLY WINTER OF 1846-47. THEY ARRIVED AT SUTTER'S FORT WITH NOTHING BUT THE CLOTHES ON THEIR BACKS. THEY WERE THE FIRST AMERICANS TO SETTLE IN SAN JUAN BAUTISTA. THEY LIVED HAPPILY EVER AFTER.

"DOLLY"

(FOR MORE ON DOLLY, SEE PAGE 60.)

"I WAS BORN UNDER AN EVIL STAR!" LEWIS KESEBERG WOULD LATER SAY OF HIS ORDEAL WITH THE DONNER PARTY. THE FINAL MEMBER TO BE RESCUED FROM TRUCKEE LAKE, HE WAS OFTEN PAINTED BY THE MEDIA AS A VILLAIN, ESPECIALLY CONCERNING THE MYSTERIOUS FATE OF TAMSEN DONNER. SOME STORIES CLAIM HE MURDERED AND ATE HER. HE WAS PLAGUED BY CANNIBAL JOKES AND RUMORS FOR THE REST OF HIS LIFE. HIS BAD LUCK CONTINUED WHEN HIS BUSINESS, A HOTEL/RESTAURANT CALLED THE LADY ADAMS, BURNED DOWN AND HIS SECOND BUSINESS, A BREWERY, WAS DESTROYED IN A FLOOD.

LEWIS KESEBERG

TO THE END OF HIS DAYS, **LANSFORD HASTINGS** INSISTED THAT HIS CUTOFF WAS THE SUPERIOR, EASIER ROUTE TO CALIFORNIA. AFTER FIGHTING IN THE MEXICAN-AMERICAN WAR, HE OFFERED TO GUIDE OTHER PIONEER GROUPS TO THE WEST. NOBODY ACCEPTED. DURING THE CIVIL WAR, HE HATCHED A PLOT TO JOIN CALIFORNIA WITH THE **SOUTH**. NOBODY ACCEPTED THAT, EITHER. HE HAD PLANS TO SET UP A COLONY IN BRAZIL FOR EXPATRIATE CONFEDERATES. ONCE AGAIN, NOBODY ACCEPTED. HE DIED ON A SHIP EN ROUTE TO BRAZIL.

HELLO, I'M NATHAN HALE
--NOT THE SPY-- THE AUTHOR OF THIS BOOK. I DREW THE PICTURES TOO.
BUT THE REAL HEART OF THIS HISTORY SERIES ISN'T THE JOKES OR THE CARTOONS.
IT'S THE RESEARCH!
MOST RESEARCH LABS EMPLOY A MIX OF LIBRARIANS, PROFESSIONAL RESEARCHERS, AND GRADUATE STUDENTS.
NOT AT HAZARDOUS TALES.
OUR RESEARCH IS COMPILED BY HUMAN BABIES.
WHY?
BECAUSE THEY ARE CUTE AS BUTTONS!
RESEARCHERS OF
AAAAAND WE CAN'T AFFORD ACTUAL GROWN-UPS.
NHHT RESEARCH LIBRARY
LET'S GO SEE WHAT THOSE CLEVER BAMBINOS ARE UP TO.
HUH?
WHERE'D THE BABIES GO?
AT LEAST THEY LEFT THE BIBLIOGRAPHY.

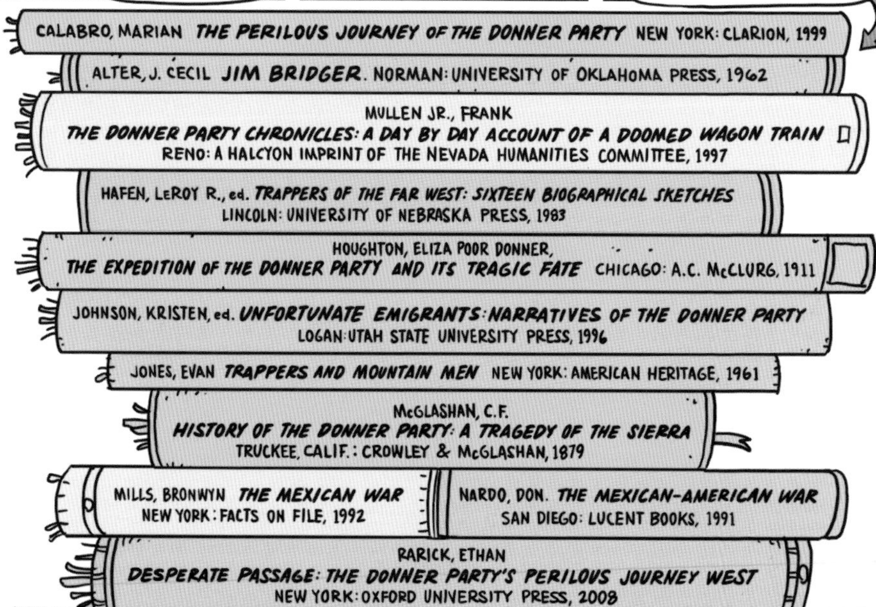
CALABRO, MARIAN THE PERILOUS JOURNEY OF THE DONNER PARTY NEW YORK: CLARION, 1999
ALTER, J. CECIL JIM BRIDGER. NORMAN: UNIVERSITY OF OKLAHOMA PRESS, 1962
MULLEN JR., FRANK THE DONNER PARTY CHRONICLES: A DAY BY DAY ACCOUNT OF A DOOMED WAGON TRAIN RENO: A HALCYON IMPRINT OF THE NEVADA HUMANITIES COMMITTEE, 1997
HAFEN, LEROY R., ed. TRAPPERS OF THE FAR WEST: SIXTEEN BIOGRAPHICAL SKETCHES LINCOLN: UNIVERSITY OF NEBRASKA PRESS, 1983
HOUGHTON, ELIZA POOR DONNER, THE EXPEDITION OF THE DONNER PARTY AND ITS TRAGIC FATE CHICAGO: A.C. McCLURG, 1911
JOHNSON, KRISTEN, ed. UNFORTUNATE EMIGRANTS: NARRATIVES OF THE DONNER PARTY LOGAN: UTAH STATE UNIVERSITY PRESS, 1996
JONES, EVAN TRAPPERS AND MOUNTAIN MEN NEW YORK: AMERICAN HERITAGE, 1961
McGLASHAN, C.F. HISTORY OF THE DONNER PARTY: A TRAGEDY OF THE SIERRA TRUCKEE, CALIF.: CROWLEY & McGLASHAN, 1879
MILLS, BRONWYN THE MEXICAN WAR NEW YORK: FACTS ON FILE, 1992
NARDO, DON. THE MEXICAN-AMERICAN WAR SAN DIEGO: LUCENT BOOKS, 1991
RARICK, ETHAN DESPERATE PASSAGE: THE DONNER PARTY'S PERILOUS JOURNEY WEST NEW YORK: OXFORD UNIVERSITY PRESS, 2008
STEWART, GEORGE R. ORDEAL BY HUNGER: THE STORY OF THE DONNER PARTY NEW YORK: HOLT, 1936
TUNIS, EDWIN FRONTIER LIVING CLEVELAND, WORLD PUB., 1961

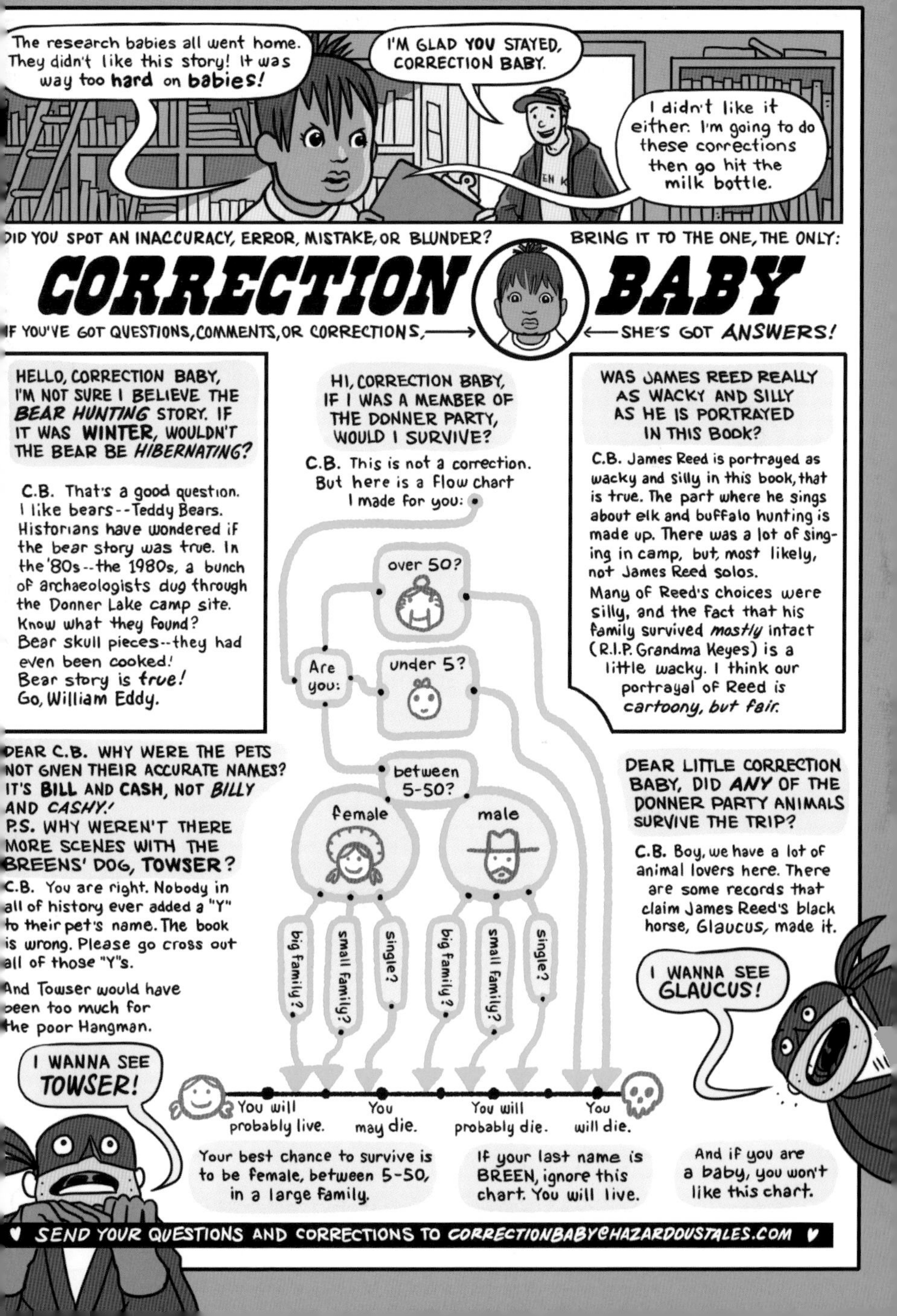
The research babies all went home. They didn't like this story! It was way too hard on babies!
I'M GLAD YOU STAYED, CORRECTION BABY.
I didn't like it either. I'm going to do these corrections then go hit the milk bottle.
DID YOU SPOT AN INACCURACY, ERROR, MISTAKE, OR BLUNDER?
BRING IT TO THE ONE, THE ONLY:
CORRECTION BABY
IF YOU'VE GOT QUESTIONS, COMMENTS, OR CORRECTIONS,
SHE'S GOT ANSWERS!
HELLO, CORRECTION BABY, I'M NOT SURE I BELIEVE THE BEAR HUNTING STORY. IF IT WAS WINTER, WOULDN'T THE BEAR BE HIBERNATING?
C.B. That's a good question. I like bears--Teddy Bears. Historians have wondered if the bear story was true. In the '80s--the 1980s, a bunch of archaeologists dug through the Donner Lake camp site. Know what they found? Bear skull pieces--they had even been cooked! Bear story is true! Go, William Eddy.
HI, CORRECTION BABY, IF I WAS A MEMBER OF THE DONNER PARTY, WOULD I SURVIVE?
C.B. This is not a correction. But here is a flow chart I made for you:
Are you:
over 50?
under 5?
between 5-50?
female
male
big family?
small family?
single?
big family?
small family?
single?
You will probably live.
You may die.
You will probably die.
You will die.
Your best chance to survive is to be female, between 5-50, in a large family.
If your last name is BREEN, ignore this chart. You will live.
And if you are a baby, you won't like this chart.
WAS JAMES REED REALLY AS WACKY AND SILLY AS HE IS PORTRAYED IN THIS BOOK?
C.B. James Reed is portrayed as wacky and silly in this book, that is true. The part where he sings about elk and buffalo hunting is made up. There was a lot of singing in camp, but, most likely, not James Reed solos. Many of Reed's choices were silly, and the fact that his family survived mostly intact (R.I.P. Grandma Keyes) is a little wacky. I think our portrayal of Reed is cartoony, but fair.
DEAR C.B. WHY WERE THE PETS NOT GIVEN THEIR ACCURATE NAMES? IT'S BILL AND CASH, NOT BILLY AND CASHY! P.S. WHY WEREN'T THERE MORE SCENES WITH THE BREENS' DOG, TOWSER?
C.B. You are right. Nobody in all of history ever added a "Y" to their pet's name. The book is wrong. Please go cross out all of those "Y"s.
And Towser would have been too much for the poor Hangman.
I WANNA SEE TOWSER!
DEAR LITTLE CORRECTION BABY, DID ANY OF THE DONNER PARTY ANIMALS SURVIVE THE TRIP?
C.B. Boy, we have a lot of animal lovers here. There are some records that claim James Reed's black horse, Glaucus, made it.
I WANNA SEE GLAUCUS!
SEND YOUR QUESTIONS AND CORRECTIONS TO CORRECTIONBABY@HAZARDOUSTALES.COM

MORE SAD AND DEPRESSING FACTS ABOUT THE DONNER PARTY
WAGON REPAIRS
HOWE BILLY THE PONEE AND CASHEE THE WEE TERRIER WOS NEVER ET
A DOG AND PONEE SHOWE BY THE HANGMAN
HALLO, THER CASHEE. ARENT YOU GLAD YOU WOS NEVER ET?
YES, BILLY, MY FREND. I AM EVERSO GLAD I WOS NOT EVER ET.
DEER FREND, SHALL WE HAV A FROLICK IN OUR BEYOOTIFULL MEDOW.
YES, IN DEED!
LOOK THERE!
WOT IS IT?
IT IS A WAGGIN FULL OF HUNGRY TRAVLERS.
OH NO! WOT IF THEY ARE HUNGRY, BILLY?
THEY WONT EAT US AGAIN!
WHY NOT?
BECOS WE WILL EAT THEM FIRST!
RARR!
GRRR!
THAT WOS A MEEL TO REMEMBER. EH CASHEE?
DEE-LISHUS!
THE END.

OH, HI THERE, I'M SUSAN B. EAGLEBEAK.
YOU MAY RECOGNIZE ME FROM THE COVER OF THIS BOOK.
WHEN I'M NOT POSING WITH FLAGS, OR FLYING MAJESICALLY OVER CRAGGY MOUNTAINS,
I'M BUSY HUNTING FOR PREY.
YOU SEE, I'M A FIERCE MOMMA EAGLE WITH TWO HUNGRY EAGLETS TO FEED.
WHEN I PICK UP DINNER--
--I ALSO LIKE TO GRAB SOME *HAZARDOUS TALES*!
OH BOY!
A JACKRABBIT CARCASS!
AWESOME! A NONFICTION, HISTORICAL, **CARTOON** ADVENTURE!
THIS ONE'S ABOUT **SPIES**! IT HAS CANNONS AND **BATTLES**, AND THE SPY NATHAN HALE'S WHOLE **BACKSTORY**!
THERE ARE SPY-CATCHERS, ELITE MILITARY UNITS, AND A COW TOTALLY **EXPLODES**! *FOR REAL!*
ONE DEAD SPY
THIS BOOK'S **CRAZY**! A GUY TRIES TO SINK A ***HUGE WAR***SHIP WITH A ***BOMB*** ON A ***STICK***!
THERE'S A CRAZY SWEDISH *INVENTOR*, A TALKING **FOX**, AND A GUY WITH A **SHARK FACE**!
BIG BAD IRONCLAD!
AMERICA MUST BE ONE *MAGICAL* PLACE!
WHERE IS AMERICA, MOM?
I DON'T KNOW. EAGLES CAN'T READ MAPS.
BUT THEY **CAN** READ *BOOKS*!
AND SMART EAGLES READ *NATHAN HALE'S HAZARDOUS TALES!*
CATCH UP ON THE WHOLE SERIES TODAY!

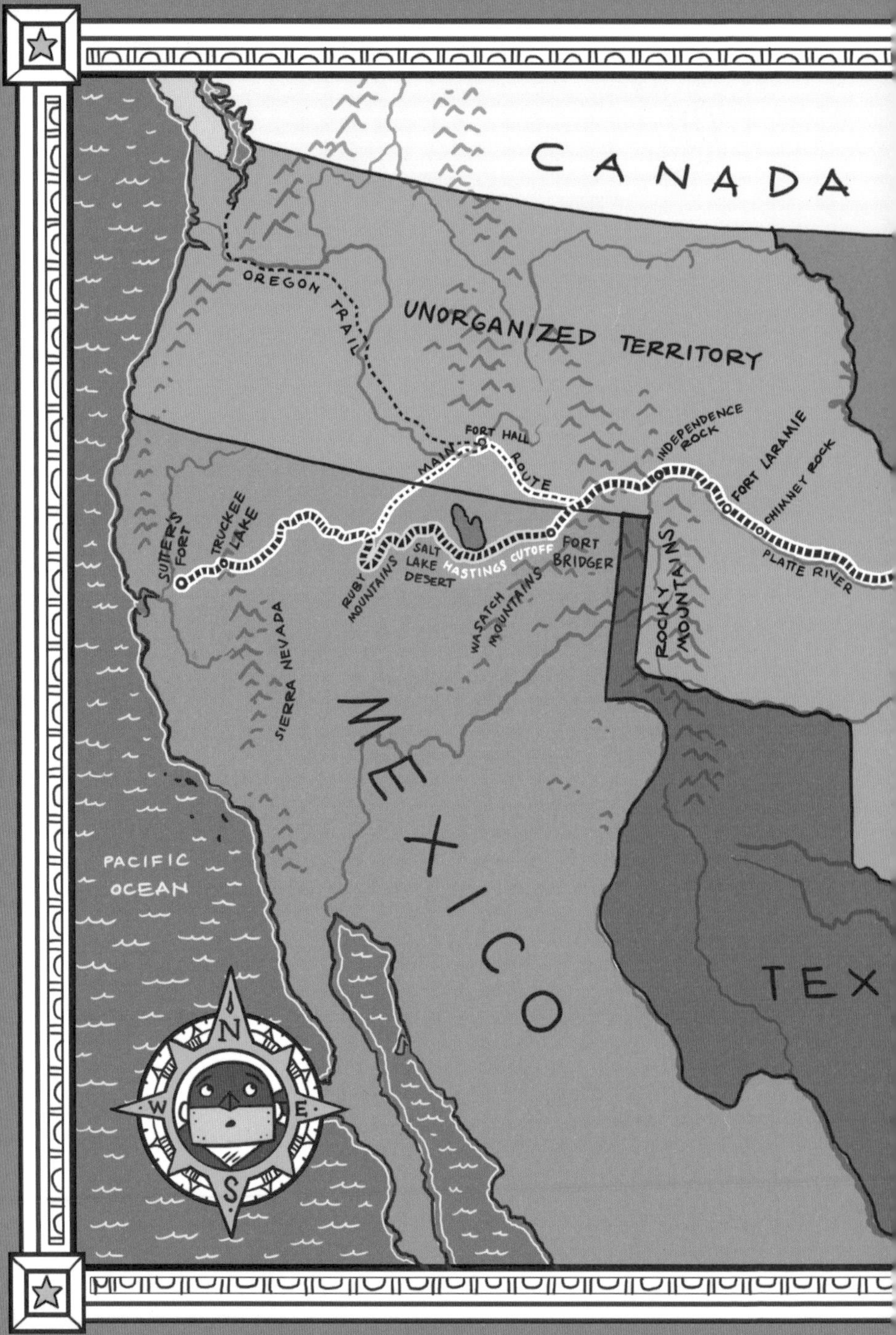
CANADA
UNORGANIZED TERRITORY
OREGON TRAIL
FORT HALL
MAIN ROUTE
INDEPENDENCE ROCK
FORT LARAMIE
CHIMNEY ROCK
PLATTE RIVER
SUTTER'S FORT
TRUCKEE LAKE
RUBY MOUNTAINS
SALT LAKE DESERT
HASTINGS CUTOFF
FORT BRIDGER
WASATCH MOUNTAINS
ROCKY MOUNTAINS
SIERRA NEVADA
MEXICO
TEX
PACIFIC OCEAN
N
S
E
W

Pest – An insect, animal, or plant that causes destruction.

Pesticide – Chemicals used to control weeds, insects, or other pests.

Planktivores – Organisms that primarily consume plankton.

Protist – An artificial classification for a group of microscopic—or nearly microscopic—single-celled organisms that are not fungi or bacteria.

Quarantine – Any system used to restrict the spread of pests or disease.

Raceme – An inflorescence characterized by having flowers arranged on the main stalk, attached on short stalks, and equidistant from each other along the main stem.

Rachis – The main stem of a leaf or inflorescence.

Reservoir – Referring to disease spread, any organism that can become infected by the pathogen.

Resistance – Plants or animals that have a genetic resistance to becoming infected.

Rhizome (and rhizomatous growth) – A horizontal, underground stem often used for plant vegetative reproduction.

Riparian – Land along the banks of rivers and streams.

Samara – A type of dry fruit containing one seed.

Sanitize – Strategies used to reduce the populations of pathogenic species.

Stolon (stoloniferous) – Horizontal plant stems growing aboveground.

Taproot – The dominant, center root of a dicot plant (e.g. a carrot is a taproot).

Tolerance – Plants or animals that can tolerate infection by a specific pathogen without experiencing severe signs and symptoms of disease.

Tympanum – The membrane that covers the ear and facilitates the conduction of sound.

Umbel – An inflorescence characterized by having flowers attached at a single point and radiating out from this point like an umbrella.

Vectors – Any organisms that facilitate the spread of a pathogenic microorganism.

Virus – A nonliving infectious agent composed of nucleic acid and a protein coat that can only reproduce inside a host cell.

Whorl (whorled) – The arrangement of plant parts (usually floral structures) that radiate from a central point.

Zoonotic – Diseases that spread between animals and humans.

Globose/Globular – More or less spherical in shape, as a globe is.

Hemiparasitic – A species that obtains some of its nutrients from other organisms.

Herbicide – Chemicals used to kill plants.

Hybridize – A plant that is the result of the pollination of one plant by another plant that is in a different taxonomic group, whether it be genus, species, variety, etc.

Infection – Referring to a successful host invasion of a pathogenic microorganism.

Infestation – Referring to uncontrolled populations of pests, including insects, plants, or animals.

Inflorescence – The arrangement of the flowers on a plant. The inflorescence can be an important identification characteristic.

Integrated pest management – A long-term strategy to reduce pathogens and pests that applies a variety of control techniques, most suited to a particular environment.

Invasive species – Non-native species that can successfully outcompete native species.

Invertebrate – An animal species that lacks a backbone, including most of the diversity in the animal kingdom.

Mechanical control – The use of manual or mechanized systems to remove pests.

Monoculture – A large area containing a single species.

Mycelium – The collective mass of hyphal strands of a fungus (long, tubular filaments) that make up the vegetative body of a fungus.

Naturalized – The ecological status describing exotic species that have developed the capacity to reproduce and spread in locations where they have been introduced.

Nematicide – Chemicals designed to kill nematodes.

Opposite – A type of leaf arrangement where two leaves are attached per node and are arranged opposite each other along the stem.

Order – A taxonomic rank above family, used in the classification of organisms.

Panicles – An inflorescence that has compound branching.

Parasite – An organism that persists by using another organism for nutrients and other aspects of survival.

Parotid gland – A structure that produces saliva in some animal species.

Pathogen – Microorganism that causes disease.

Perennial – A plant that persists for more than two growing seasons.

GLOSSARY

Allelopath – The ability of a plant to restrict the growth and reproduction of neighboring plants through the production of inhibitory chemicals.

Alternate – A leaf arrangement where one leaf is attached per node on alternating sides.

Annual – A plant that completes its entire life cycle in one growing season.

Bacteria – Single-celled organisms that lack a nucleus or other membrane-bound organelles.

Ballast water – Water brought on board a ship to balance its weight and provide stability.

Biennial – A plant that completes its life cycle over two growing seasons.

Bilateral symmetry – Structures that can be divided into two identical halves.

Biodiversity – The variety of species located in a particular habitat.

Biological control – The use of living organisms, or the products of living organisms, to control invasive species, pests, or pathogens.

Canker – A sunken, often oozing wound observed in some diseased plants.

Chemical control – The use of chemicals to control invasive species, pests, or pathogens.

Culm – The stem of a plant in the grass family.

Cultivar – An abbreviation for a "cultivated variety" of a crop plant.

Deciduous – Plants, typically trees, that seasonally lose their leaves.

Defoliated – The loss of all plant leaves, often due to disease or pests.

Eradicated – The elimination of all unwanted species in an area.

Evergreen – A plant that remains green during the entire year.

Exotic species – Organisms that have been introduced into new ecosystems beyond their native range.

Extirpation – The extinction of a species or population from an area.

Forb – A nonwoody flowering plant, not including grass species.

Fungus – A group of multicellular organisms with cell walls that contain chitin and that reproduce by spores. Some fungi produce mushrooms.

Galleries – Tunnels made by some insect pests that can serve as signs of infestation.

Genus – A hierarchical taxonomic rank above species.

Girdle – Cutting bark in a ring around the entire circumference of a tree to inhibit the flow of sugar and ultimately kill the tree.

farms and hatcheries. Some salmonid species are more resistant than others and may be used to breed more resistant strains of susceptible species. Certain drugs have been shown to significantly lower infection rates, but they are only used in aquacultural settings, not in the wild. Public education and regulations focused on preventing the transport of fish and bait from one water body to another are other tactics.

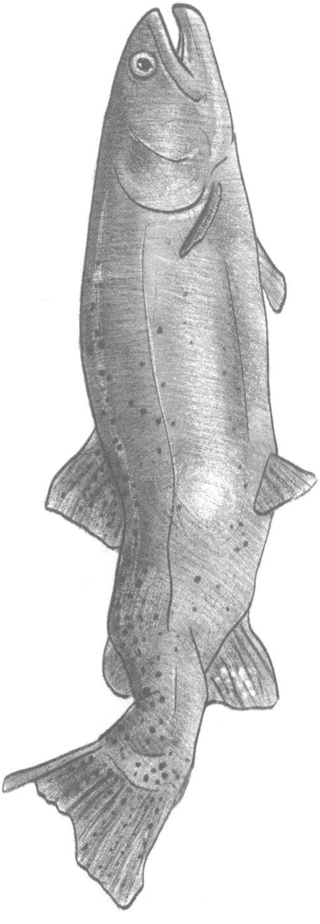

Myxobolus cerebralis

WHIRLING DISEASE

DESCRIPTION: This species is a microscopic parasite of wild and aquacultured salmonid fish. It has a complex life cycle, including two different hosts: salmonid fish and tube worms. It causes Whirling Disease in the fish, which affects their skeletal and nervous systems. This disease causes infected fish to swim in a "whirling" manner, with a mortality rate of up to 90 percent. Those fish that do survive still act as a reservoir for the parasite.

NATIVE DISTRIBUTION: It is believed to be native to Europe and western Russia, although it is difficult to determine precisely where it is considered native. It was first discovered in Germany in the late 1890s.

NORTH AMERICAN DISTRIBUTION: It can be found in Canada and the United States, although the extent is difficult to determine accurately. It has been reported from at least 20 states.

DATE(S) AND MEANS OF INTRODUCTION: It was first confirmed in Nevada and Pennsylvania in the 1950s. It may have been present in New York in the 1930s, but this cannot be confirmed. It has spread primarily through the commerce of live fish and eggs, fish stocking practices, and frozen fish for the market. The parasite can also be transported in water, sediment, and fish-eating organisms, such as birds and mammals.

THREATS: The parasite can significantly impact the local population of salmonid fish. In aquaculture settings, the parasite can spread quickly, causing the death of all fish that may have encountered the infected fish, resulting in significant financial losses for the aquaculture industry. It may also impact fishery quality, ultimately leading to a decline in tourism and subsequent economic impacts.

MANAGEMENT: Aquacultural practices have been implemented that are designed to stop the spread of the parasite. These practices have been relatively successful, and the parasite has been eliminated from many fish

Alexandrium minutum

PARALYTIC SHELLFISH POISONING (PSP)

DESCRIPTION: *Alexandrium minutum* is a dinoflagellate (one-celled, flagellated alga) that produces a biotoxin. When filter-feeding shellfish consume *A. minutum*, the shellfish also acquire the toxin.

NATIVE DISTRIBUTION: It was first reported in Egypt in 1960.

NORTH AMERICAN DISTRIBUTION: *Alexandrium minutum* is considered cosmopolitan.

DATE(S) AND MEANS OF INTRODUCTION: Unknown.

THREATS: The most significant danger is to human health and safety. Consuming shellfish containing the PSP toxin causes severe illness or death. In some fatal cases, the victim may stop breathing due to paralysis of the muscles responsible for breathing. Usually, symptoms are experienced within an hour of eating shellfish containing PSP. Although fatalities are rare, they are increasing. As global ocean temperatures rise, populations of *A. minutum* have increased. The incidence of PSP has increased by 3.5 times in self-harvested shellfish over the last decade.

MANAGEMENT: The Centre for Agriculture and Bioscience International (CABI) reports that control of *A. minutum* to prevent PSP "appears to be almost impossible." In dormancy, the algae produce a tough, single-celled cyst that is readily carried in ballast water to new locations. Exposure to PSP toxins can be prevented by only consuming shellfish that has been tested for toxins. Consuming shellfish from noncommercial or self-harvested sources increases the likelihood of exposure to PSP toxins.

OTHERS

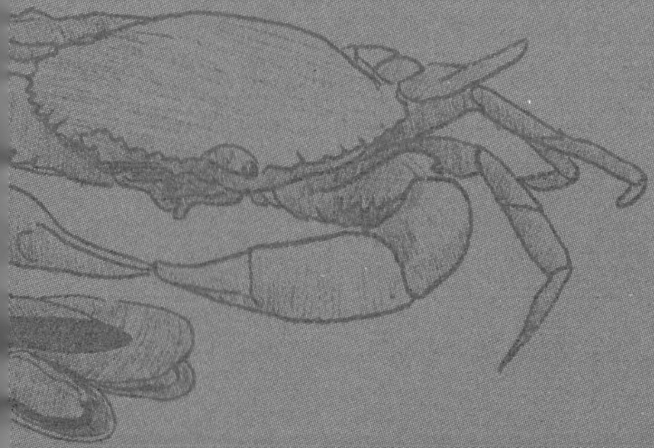